TAUGHT

TAUGHT

A Memoir and Educator's Guide to Classroom Transformation and Student Liberation

BY KELLEY POMIS

Teacher Renewed

CONTENTS

Paperback: 978-1-7923-8958-0
EBook: 978-1-7923-8959-7

Edited by Sia Henry
Printed by IngramSpark,USA

Introduction

Dear Reader,

For seven years I taught students in some of the most under-resourced communities in North Carolina. While I was able to lead my students to achieve amazing academic results based on state testing outcomes, over time I realized (far later than I should have) my tactics were often oppressive, fueled by a sense of urgency and unconscious bias.

Taught captures the stories of my time as a classroom teacher, teacher coach, school board member, school administrator, and education advocate. This book highlights my experiences working primarily with students of color, and my unconscious perpetuation of oppressive and racist practices. In addition to stories, I share the lessons I came to learn, chronicled through letters to my students (my ultimate teachers and whose names I have changed because while this book does not capture me in the prettiest ways initially, they deserve the utmost respect). Ultimately, it is my hope that my reflections will inspire and support the development of teachers facing the all-too-familiar learning opportunities that come with being a teacher, particularly a white teacher, in predominantly marginalized communities of color.

In the years I began coaching teachers I often said, "my goal is to ensure you don't do what I did!" As my teachers confronted challenges similar to ones I have faced, I would share with them the approaches I employed and we would collaborate to identify anti-oppressive and anti-racist alternatives. For over a decade, as a teacher coach, I have helped transform hundreds of classrooms, ensuring teachers show up in the ways their students need them to. I coached from a place of learning and humility and saw teachers progress much more quickly than I did as an educator. For most of my teachers, as they began to rely on culturally thoughtful and relational strategies in their classrooms, their students soared.

In *Taught* I share some of the most humbling, oftentimes cringe-worthy, stories of my time as a classroom teacher. Most of all, I reflect on what I learned and ways to overcome, if not avoid, harmful situations like the ones I created, specifically through leveraging relationships with students and families and building a strong and loving classroom culture.

Taught shares a critical message, not only given the United States' history of oppression and racial and social injustice, but also given the state of education in this country. Currently in the US, 80% of teachers are white while nearly 56% of students are students of color (Meckler & Robinowitz, 2019). This disparity often results in challenges, toxic interactions, and a strong likelihood teachers are perpetuating direct and generational harms and trauma. Researchers have found both "evidence of systematic bias in teacher expectations for African American students" as well as non-black teachers holding "lower expectations of black students than black teachers" (Gerchenson, 2018).

This all has long-term, negative effects on students of color. As the diversity of the students in this country continues to grow, it is vital our teaching practices acknowledge and honor our students' backgrounds and lived experiences. Our educators must not only be willing to examine their implicit and explicit biases but also forge practices that dismantle racism and oppression in educational spaces to give all of their students the healthy and transformative education they deserve.

Taught explores what these practices could look like in the classroom. These concrete resources are imperative as too many teachers are entering the profession neither emotionally nor technically equipped to teach in ways that are sustainable for them and healthy for their students. According to the National Center for Education Statistics (NCES, 2014), each year, 8% of teachers leave the profession and another 8% move to other schools, bringing the total annual turnover rate to 16%. That means that on average, a school will lose approximately three out of every 20 teachers each year. To make matters worse, nearly 50% of new teachers leave the profession within their first five years (USDOE, 2011).

Even more staggering are the rates teachers are leaving the profession in schools considered to be in low-income and/ or racially diverse areas. University of Pennsylvania Professor Richard Ingersoll's research shows underserved schools lose 20% of their faculty each year. For example, in New York

City, approximately two-thirds of educators (66%) change careers within the first five years of teaching (2018). Therefore, teachers in diverse and/or low-income areas are leaving at an increased rate of 32% compared to the national average. According to the University of Chicago's Urban Education Institute, some underserved schools even lose half of their teaching staff every three years. (Allensworth, Ponosciak, & Mazzeo, 2009)

While challenging work conditions and pay are often named as primary reasons educators are leaving the profession, one of the greatest contributing factors is the lack of support systems in the nascent years of teachers' careers. Teachers feeling supported and having a community they can rely on are factors instrumental to keeping them in the classroom. This, in turn, benefits students as they are able to learn and grow in spaces led by dedicated and experienced educators.

The stories in this book are not only meant to help teachers learn from harmful mistakes I made but also serve as a guide to combat the pervasive challenges of keeping good teachers in classrooms by providing support, care, and tangible ways to improve their practices.

Our country is in a crisis to not only find great teachers but also retain them. To retain them we must ensure they are cognizant of practices that impede their students' learning and potentially harmful biases they might have. They also need support to combat those biases and implement best practices.

My hope is that *Taught* serves as a source of reflection and inspiration and includes tangible methods to ensure any teacher, particularly those who are white teaching in racially diverse schools, can create a foundation of transformation for themselves and liberation for their students.

With Humility and Hope,

KP

1

Mistakes: I've Made Quite a Few! But You Don't Have To

My First Year: Can I Have a Do-Over?

Most, if not all, first-year teachers have aspirational visions of what their classroom will look and feel like. I was no exception as I set out across the country from Colorado Springs, CO to Rocky Mount, NC. Along my journey to my inaugural teaching experience, I daydreamed about meeting my students at the door and giving them high fives, hugs, or hand shakes. As I drove over 1,000 miles, I pictured my students starting their mornings with large smiles and going about their days with joy, love, and a zest for learning. I anticipated being the one to inspire my group of middle school students with behavioral and emotional disabilities (BED) to achieve greatness. I assumed the realities of the lack of success they had had in school since first coming into contact with public education would melt away. I ended my first day of teaching thinking this all might actually happen. Then day two began.

The first words I heard from a student on my second day as a teacher were, "Ms. Teacher, I haven't had breakfast." The second set of words I heard from a student were "fuck you."

At that point, the school had moved my students (12 sixth- and seventh-grade boys), Ms. L (my classroom assistant), and me from our initial classroom (the teacher's former smoking lounge turned storage room). Given this classroom barely fit my original six students before our group doubled in size, it was clear we needed a new classroom. We had spent the first day of the school year packing up our things and moving to a slightly larger room, which was now the former in-school suspension (ISS) room.

It appeared on that second day my students could not find our new classroom as breakfast was ending, the first bell was about to ring, and I still did not see any of my assigned students. I finally spotted one of my sixth graders, Jamar, coming down the hall. He looked bewildered, and rightfully so. Not only had he just started middle school the day before, he had spent the second half of his fifth-grade year in a hospital dealing with mental health issues. He was required to have an adult shadowing him at all times. Jamar's shadow, however, had not yet clocked in.

Walking into the classroom, Jamar informed me he had not yet eaten breakfast. As a two-day-old teacher, I had no clue what to do. I told Jamar to find his seat and I would figure out how to ensure he ate. Luckily, at that moment, the principal happened to be walking past.

"Ah Ms. A!" I exclaimed, "Can I ask you a quick question?"

"Quickly!" she replied.

"I have a student who came to class first but still needs to eat breakfast. His shadow is not here yet to help him. What should I do?"

She walked past me and told Jamar to look at her. "You're in middle school now," she proclaimed. "That means you need to know this for yourself! Just like we have been communicating all summer and in all of our orientations, when you get to school, you need to go straight to the cafeteria and get your breakfast." She turned around and walked out the door.

Given the circumstances around Jamar re-entering public school, I wasn't sure if he had ever attended an orientation. I hadn't.

Upon the principal's exit, Jamar folded his arms on his desk, buried his head in them, and began pounding his fists.

With shaky nerves I walked to my desk, grabbed the granola bar I had brought for my own breakfast, and offered it to Jamar. He yelled, "Fuck you!" as he smacked away my hand.

This outburst happened as Ms. L walked in with the rest of the students.

"Ahhhhh" erupted from my students, hands circling their mouths and waving in the air. One of my sixth graders, Derrick, asked, "What did you do to him?"

Telling the boys to get to their seats, Ms. L walked over to me to find out what was going on. Jamar, overhearing us, began scribbling on his desk with his pencil, his head still buried in his arms. I wish I could say a few minutes of peace and being left alone was all he needed. Perhaps a walk and the promise of breakfast. Things, however, only escalated and Ms. L told me we needed to get the rest of the students out of the room.

Mustering as much confidence as I could, I said, "Alright boys, we are stepping out now. So come on!"

They reluctantly followed. While in the hallway, Jamar's shadow finally arrived and the boys were all too eager to let her know what was happening.

Shortly after she entered the classroom to speak to Jamar alongside Ms. L, shouting began and it was clear furniture was being thrown. While I tried to manage my other students, now standing around in the hallway, the School Resource Officer (SRO)[1] arrived and went into the room.

[1] A school resource officer is a sworn law-enforcement officer with arrest powers who works, either full or part time, in a school setting.

There was more yelling, more rustling of furniture, and approximately ten minutes later the commotion subsided. The door finally opened. Jamar was handcuffed and the SRO escorted him out of the room. That was the last time the class and I ever saw Jamar. It was only my second day of teaching and I had already lost one student.

For most of the third day of school the students did well. Toward the end of the day, however, something happened between two students, Charles and Kamal. I can't recall what prompted the exchange, but one asked, "You want to go?" and the other lunged.

Ms. L jumped in the middle and managed to hold Charles back. Once again, not knowing what to do, Ms. L told me to call the SRO. When he arrived, arguing ensued and while the SRO remained calm, the students' tempers rose. I was able to get Kamal out of the room and had him come on a brief walk with me while Ms. L kept an eye on the rest of the class. The SRO stayed behind to talk to Charles.

As soon as Kamal and I returned, Charles bound once more at Kamal. The SRO stepped in this time, trying to restrain Charles. Charles yelled, "Get your hands off of me!" And ran out the door with the SRO following him.

At the end of the day, when the class and I walked to dismissal, we noticed Charles running around the school buses with the SRO calmly following him. Leaving the class with Ms. L, I went outside and pleaded, "Charles, please come with me! The buses are about to leave and I just want you to be safe!" To my surprise, he came. We walked back into the school together and were told to wait in the office while the admin called his mom.

While we waited I asked Charles what happened. No words came out, he simply broke down and cried. Unexpectedly, he buried himself in my hug and continued to cry. When his mom arrived, she said, "I am done! I don't know what to do with this child. Nothing is working." The principal informed Charles's mom that they were suspending him due to insubordination and he could return to school the following Monday. That was the last time my students and I ever saw Charles.

Luckily, Kamal and Charles's fight never escalated into a physical altercation and Kamal returned to school the next day.

Day four was calmer but still eventful. I was going over math problems with a small group of my seventh graders, while some students worked independently and another small group worked with Ms. L. All seemed fine until one of my sixth graders, Chris, raised his hand and asked, "Can I move? Mike said he was going to kill me."

"Ummm.... sure?" I replied and asked Mike, a seventh grader, "Did you say that?"

"Yeah! He was humming and getting on my nerves."

In Mike's hand were a pair of scissors. Despite my requests, demands, and pleading, Mike would not hand over the scissors. This time, Ms. L called the SRO. He came and escorted Mike out of the room. Fortunately, Mike eventually returned to class, but that was not the last of the challenges he endured as a seventh grader that year.

Before I left school that fourth day, all three administrators sat Ms. L and me down and said, "Your students are too much of a nuisance and a distraction to the rest of the students who are here to learn." They decided to move us, once again, this time outside of the main building to a trailer. They also informed us we needed to rely less on the SRO as there were other needs in the school besides my students'.

As I moved everything to our third classroom for the week, I was determined to prove myself to my students and the administration. I stayed late into the night helping the custodians move desks, an old chalkboard, two computers, and the rest of the materials and resources I had already set up twice before.

That Friday morning, while I was putting the final touches on our new classroom, I heard a ruckus outside. One student exclaimed, "Ahhhhh hell no! Another trailer! You better be kidding! That's what they always do to us!"

I opened the door to greet the boys and Ms. L but Nic

interrupted exclaiming, "Nope! I ain't going in! Every year they put us in a trailer."

The rest of the boys slowly shuffled in and found their desks as Ms. L eventually got Nic to come inside. I thought if we could just get to the lesson we could move on from the latest transition, not realizing my haste to "push through" meant I was ultimately ignoring my students' need to process and talk about their frustrations. The "lesson" itself did not go well as the boys' anxiety and irritation went unaddressed. No real learning happened that day, nor did real restorative processes.

That was week one. Week two had to be better, right? It wasn't.

Monday of the second week of school, one of my sixth graders, William, did not show up for class. Well into the morning lesson, we heard a knock and the door flew open. A woman I didn't recognize entered along with William trailing behind her. Apparently William had gotten into a fight on the bus so the bus driver pulled over and kicked William off. William, being resourceful, walked to his former elementary school, where he found his former teacher who drove him to school.

We got William settled and then the previous teacher and I walked to the front office. In the conference room, sitting alongside the school admin and sixth-grade counselor, I learned quite a bit about William, including the many hardships he had endured. I learned about the on-again, off-again relationship he had with his Attention Deficit and Hyperactivity Disorder (ADHD) medicine. I also learned about his similarly sporadic relationship with his mother, which meant a back-and-forth relationship he had with the foster care system. William had been receiving support services since before he entered kindergarten. He began receiving special education (SPED) services in the Learning Disabled (LD) and Behavioral and Emotional Disabilities (BED) categories.

I returned to my class to finish out the day's lesson but, later that afternoon, I was called back down to the office. I was informed William would be riding the SPED bus (otherwise known as "the short bus") indefinitely.

The next day, the seventh day of my teaching career, I woke up believing things could only get better. In hindsight, I was delusional. That Tuesday, two new challenges arose that I could not have prepared for.

Challenge 1: Derrick was sent back to class from Physical Education (PE) for fighting with another student. The administration decided to suspend him for three days and revoke his right to Elective classes indefinitely, which meant he would be in my class all day, every day. Instead of accepting this severe punishment, Derrick's mom pulled him out of the school.

Challenge 2: William was also sent out of PE but not for

fighting. As Ms. L took care of the situation with Derrick, I went to the office to retrieve William. When I arrived, not only was I greeted by a very upset assistant principal, but also a pungent smell. It so happened that William's mom had both punished William the night before and found his ADHD medication and forced him to take it before coming to school. I don't know the extent of the punishment the previous night, all I know is that day at school, William defecated on himself, leaving a trail from the office entrance to the staff bathroom. We informed his mom, who responded, "It happened at school. Not my problem."

* * *

I lost two students in my first two weeks as a teacher. By the end of the semester, my original class of twelve students with Behavioral and Emotional Disabilities had been whittled down to five.

Jamar: never returned after what happened the second day of school.

Charles: never returned after the third day of school.

Mike: was expelled for selling drugs at school.

William: was expelled for bringing a knife to school and threatening a student with it.

Kamal: his parents were in and out of the prison system and when both were reincarcerated, he moved to live with his grandparents.

Derrick: his mom initially pulled him from the school and I later found out his family was evicted and our school was not in fact his "home" school.

I lost a lot that year: students, battles, belief, hope, pride. Those losses, especially the circumstances around them, however, pushed me to learn a lot. Namely, I gained humility, hope, belief, an understanding of what true advocacy looks like, and so much more.

My Letter

To all the students I lost my first year of teaching,

I am sorry. Over the past two decades I have learned a lot about myself and what I would have done differently in those first few days and weeks of school and what I commit to doing differently now.

Not knowing how important relationships and classroom culture were, I thought I needed to jump into teaching curriculum immediately without knowing your learning needs and/or the approximate grade levels you were performing at, not to mention getting to know you as individuals. This meant the first few days of school I was giving you content that (1) meant little to you and (2) you were not academically ready to learn.

Instead of trying to get to know you and working on ways to deescalate situations, I called the SRO on some of you and allowed you to be treated like criminals. I supported the administration's decisions for your suspensions and transfers instead of advocating for you to remain in my classroom. I opted for outcomes that were "easier for me" versus ones that were better for your lives. For so many of you, you were prescribed medicine to "calm" your energy so you could be more focused. When you came to school without your medicine, instead of providing you space to exert your energy, I confined and isolated you to study desks. Often, I didn't give you an appropriate outlet, causing you to engage in behavior that ultimately resulted in a suspension and mandated meetings seeking "better" environments for you (aka removal from our community).

Here's what I wish I had done:

Jamar- I wish I would have never involved the principal and instead had simply told you, "When Ms. L or your shadow get here, we will go to the cafeteria to get you breakfast so that you know where to go tomorrow."

Charles- I wish I would have understood your tears as a sign of remorse and said, "Let him be at school tomorrow.

Ms. L and I can find a way to keep him and the other student apart and when the time is right, we can bring them together to have a restorative conversation."

Mike- Your mom advocated for and loved you so much. Instead of agreeing with the school's administration that it might be in your best interest to be transferred to another program at another school, I should have said, "Let's make some changes and see if these changes lead to more success. Trust that I've got yours and your mom's backs."

William- I wish I would have ensured you were seeing a school counselor regularly and given you the time and space you needed to process the trauma you had endured throughout your life. The resources were all around me but I never utilized them to their capabilities. You deserved so much more from me. Instead of advocating for you to have access to those resources, we shortened your day and treated you like a student who didn't have the ability to function in the world. While I know the circumstances of your life made success challenging for you, as I reflect back, I believe in all my heart that, with the right resources, you could have thrived at school.

Kamal- I don't ultimately know where you went, but I know it involved living without your parents and required you to move to a different town. I remember the strides you were making and most importantly your love for checkers and chess. These games were your de-escalation. I remember how hard it was for you to read but how seamless it was for you to see five moves ahead when playing a game of chess. I wish we had more time to see what could have come out of that year.

Derrick- I remember first meeting you and watching you pick up a baby out of a stroller and making her giggle and laugh. I thought the baby was your sister. I asked you her name, you shrugged and said "I don't know." I looked at the woman pushing the stroller thinking maybe she knew you and asked, "How long have the two of you known each other?" Laughing, she responded, "I am meeting him for the first time right now." You had this beautiful way of breaking the ice and making people smile. While I don't know where you ended up, I wish I could have supported you through your exit from the program because, in my heart, I know SPED was not the right environment for you. You self-regulated, you worked to improve when redirected, and you worked hard on your work.

It should not have taken me so long to realize all of the above and I should and could have advocated for you all differently. For years, I never dreamt of wanting to go back to endure that first year again but now, more than ever, I wish I could because you would have had a different teacher and a different educational experience. I would have advocated like hell to keep you in the classroom and I would have found more ways for each of you to be successful.

I can't go back but, moving forward, for all the students I

work with now and for all teachers I support, they will know the teacher you deserved then is the educator I am committed to being each and every day!

With regret and love,

Ms. (Adams) Pomis

Lessons and Resources

Put learning about and knowing your students first
Had I spent that first week starting to understand each of my students, getting to know who they were, what made them tick, what academic levels they were entering the school year at, I would not have found out the hard way. By "the hard way" I mean students acting out because they felt they couldn't do something or did not have the coping mechanisms to support their emotions. As teachers, in your first few weeks of school, it is imperative to build in time to talk one on one with students, infuse culture-building activities that align and support your vision for the classroom, and include ample "getting to know each other" activities so you are cultivating a culture of trust. Also, be sure you prioritize diagnostics in those first few weeks of school. As you are making your first 30-day plans, be sure to know what your school uses to assess your students' learning levels, when you will assess the data,

and how to interpret the data so that when you are building content you have ways to make it accessible to all of your students. (You can find a First 15 Day Plan on the resources page of www.teacherrenewed.com.)

Give yourself permission to prioritize classroom culture

I was so set on teaching content in that first semester. I thought when a student exhibited behavior indicating they didn't "want" to learn on a given day, that day was lost. I would then isolate the student and essentially leave them "alone" while they slept, colored, drew... basically anything that kept them quiet. Initially, in those moments, I didn't think I could help and actually engage them in learning.

Committed to changing my experience and theirs, in our second semester I actually put culture first and, instead of diving right into content each day, we began with check-ins to see where students' emotional needs were. I also amped up the incentives in the classroom where students would work for computer game time, cafeteria lunches, chess, classroom celebrations, recess (despite being in middle school), helping in the classroom of students with severe mental disabilities, and so many other things that mattered to my students. By shifting the focus from "covering" content to building culture, my students actually began to learn more content. Had I known how important culture building (inclusive of internalizing clear expectations, procedures, and mindsets) was to the learning outcomes of my students, we would not have lost so much learning time during those first semesters.

Utilize and** advocate like hell for the **resources around you

As a first-year teacher, I really had no clue what resources were available and, if I did know they existed, I did not know how to use them. As I reflect on that first year, my school had three counselors, all of whom I could have utilized to support the emotional needs of my students. Not once did I send my students to the counselor's office and/or set up regular check-ins. If your school has counselors and your students need their services, talk to your students' families and secure time and space for them to access this much-needed emotional and mental support. If your school does not have counselors, I can almost guarantee you will find supportive services in your community, often free to the school and covered by Medicaid or other forms of your students' family's insurance. Simply look up "behavioral health services in my area" and you will likely find something. If nothing else, most if not all schools/districts have school psychologists who can offer referrals.

For all of the school counselors I have met, none entered into the profession to be glorified college and career counselors nor to be test coordinators. Had I utilized the counselors, my students could have received much-needed services. We also had a school social worker who was at the school at least once a week. I met her once when Ms. L noticed the boys needed new shoes. The social worker found a way to get each student a new pair. That was the only time we relied on the social worker's services. I now know when I couldn't get a hold of Kamal's family that first month of school, the social worker could have taken me on a home visit. If you have a social worker or community advocate/team at your school and have students with needs that could be met by the services they provide, I encourage you to set up a monthly check-in with them as they will likely provide you immense insight in how they can support your students and your students' families.

CHAPTER 2

Going Overboard with Consequences

When a student can quote Charlie Daniels, a teacher knows that student is going to be "special." I can't say I knew who Charlie Daniels was when I asked Jay where he learned that from. And by "that" I mean he was running around the playground saying to his classmates, "I told you once you son of a bitch!"

I met Jay in my fifth year of teaching. By that point I was a "general education" teacher working with first and second graders. Jay was and still is one of the most vibrant students I ever taught. As a second grader, he was new to the school. He came from a household where both parents had good, steady jobs. He had a younger, preschool-age sister. He played sports on the weekends and I even attended a few of his games. And yes, he clearly knew the more "colorful" words from the song, "The Devil Went Down to Georgia."

Jay was also bright and sociable. So bright that I wasn't always sure what to do with him as he was above grade level in both reading and math, unlike the majority of my students who entered my 1st/2nd grade combined class on average at a kindergarten academic level. He was so sociable, it seemed every minute he was chatting away with his peers. He often had time to do so because he would complete his work quickly. "Thinkshop" was a part of class where students could work independently or in small groups on various forms of work. What would take the rest of the class one to two weeks to complete would take Jay one to two days. The mechanics and creativity in his writing were aspirational. He truly was a brilliant young person.

Because the school was relatively fluid in our approach to education, Jay was able to join the 3rd/4th grade class for math and was also in a small reading group in my class where he and two other peers who read at similar levels were able to select books of their choice and read them together. This approach to reading was beneficial to Jay only initially as he quickly became bored.

Jay, like many other second graders, was happiest at recess. He would run and play to his heart's content. Tag was his favorite. He had energy like no one else and this energy spilled over in the classroom. When finished with his work, it seemed he was a buzz; scurrying around, talking to anyone who would listen. While there was always plenty of work to do, he quickly completed it and would continue to move about the classroom, which I found to be "disrespectful" and "distracting."

In the years preceding, I had visited a school where they had something called "bench." This was essentially a consequence system where seats were taken away from students who could not stay in them or had done something "wrong." Seeing this, I was inspired. I thought this would be great for Jay. If he couldn't stay in his seat then I would take it away. I *never* considered how inhumane this "consequence" was and certainly never considered how it would make Jay, his family, my colleagues, and students feel. In my mind it was what he needed. After a few days, I remember offering his chair back, but he refused, not out of joy in the freedom of standing but out of protest against me and the oppressive nature in which I took his chair. He was now "choosing" to stand in order to protest my now desire for him to sit.

In between the time I took the chair away and his refusal to accept it back I received a letter from Jay's dad. I can't recall all that the letter said but it was nearly a full page explaining how horrific and oppressive the consequence of taking a chair away was. I also recall the letter describing what it meant for a parent to hear their child was being treated that way. Shamefully, I read the letter but never followed-up with Jay's father. Instead of confronting the situation, providing his family space to be heard and share their thoughts and feelings and even choice in the matter, I never looked at the letter again. The letter made an important point and while I never took another child's chair away, unfortunately, I hadn't learned my lesson yet.

My Letter

Jay,

When I reminisce about my students and their families, you and yours come to mind often. As a second grader, your mind was creative, your spirit vibrant, and energy infectious.

I am not sure if you remember your second-grade year but, in retrospect, I know I did not make it easy for you. When you expressed your creativity, vibrancy, and energy, I would hand you a consequence, be that not playing with your friends at recess or taking away your chair in class.

Instead of trying to repress your incredible attributes, I should have found more ways to embrace them and provide you with more outlets to engage in them.

Your parents were (likely still are) incredible advocates whose voices I neglected to hear because I didn't want to be called out for my actions. I am not sure if you remember when your dad wrote me a letter about me taking your chair away. He explained why my actions were wrong, not just for you but for any child. The letter was impactful in that it high-lighted my actions as oppressive. While I cannot recollect all he said in that letter, I can still recall shaking as I read it and wanting to defend my actions despite having no reasonable justification for my behavior. You deserved better and your family knew that. Other students in the class deserved better and your family knew that. I should have known that and even if I did, my actions did not indicate it.

Jay, I hope you know how much you and your family taught me and I hope you know that as I continue to work in education, I use those lessons daily.

You and your family reminded me that students are human and deserve to be treated as such. I should never have needed that reminder in my teaching career, but you all gave me a hard and much needed wake-up call.

You and your family remind me (daily, believe it or not) the importance of forming genuine and authentic relationships with students and their families. I often wonder how differently I would have treated you and how you could have thrived in my class had I built and supported a more meaningful relationship with you and your family.

You and your family taught me students are other people's children. If a family feels wronged, teachers must listen and cannot be defensive. It is not our job to defend our oppressive actions, it is our job to love and support our students in all that they are and bring to this world. This realization has become even clearer as I am now a mom of two boys (who are very similar to the eight-year-old you were). It should

NEVER take an educator becoming a parent or guardian to learn this lesson.

Your family taught me my vision for a well-behaved class was not one that would positively impact the lives of my students. Educators have to be aware of their biases and consider how they impact their students' learning. You were well above grade level in all academic areas and had energy that didn't fit the "mold" of who I wanted my students to be while in my classroom. I had some pretty serious, negative biases toward any student who was not "compliant." I have since learned, with the help of you and your family, "compliance" should NEVER be the end goal in a classroom. Too often, students of color and those otherwise considered to be "outside the margins" are expected to simply assimilate into mainstream, white culture. While this expectation of conformity dates back well before our modern system of education, it became even more pervasive once integration started. I have learned non-compliance is not necessarily a "bad" thing, it's all about perspective. We should be giving students opportunities to engage meaningfully and excitedly in their learning, communicate with peers, use their imagination, and form their own opinions. You had the ability to do all of this but I was more focused on you sitting down and learning the way I wanted you and the rest of the class to learn.

Thank you for these lessons in helping me understand there are so many other ways to support students. I carry you and your family in my mind and heart and felt the need to share this with you.

I hope the year you spent in my classroom did not have too much of a negative impact on your amazing energy. I also hope throughout your K-12 education experience you had teachers who embraced the spirited, vibrant, brilliant human you are.

Embracing all of this now (and hoping it is not too late),

Ms. Adams

Lessons and Resources

Restorative and collaborative practices far outweigh any consequence

In writing this letter to Jay I realized I never had closure. I recall reading Jay's dad's letter and, knowing what I know now, I wish with all of my heart that I had reached out. More than anything, I wish I had treated Jay better. I wish I had known taking a student's chair away and making them stand all day is not okay. I should have known. But I didn't. Because I had seen this done in a school that I and many of my peers held in high regard, I did not think to question whether it was right. I also never thought about talking to Jay to find out how he felt about the situation. It didn't occur to me to find out from him what he needed to be more successful in the classroom. I only saw a student being noncompliant, not meeting my expectations. I therefore resorted to punitive consequences. Before taking Jay's chair, I am sure I had other conversations with him to try to change his unwanted behavior, but I did not collaborate with his family, who would have been more than willing to work alongside me to ensure Jay had the support and environment he needed.

If at any time a consequence is warranted, reach out to the family. Work with them to realize healthier outcomes that benefit both the student and the classroom environment. More than anything, be sure to have a restorative conversation with the student. The restorative approach is a way of working with conflict that puts the focus on repairing the harm that has been done. This is not a one-way approach where you as the educator are telling the student what they did wrong. Instead, this method ensures all parties, both teacher and student(s), discuss their role in harm caused, the causes, and how the incident or conflict has affected them. Everyone involved in the conversation then comes to an agreement about what needs to be done for things to be put right. This approach not only helps students understand consequences, if warranted, but more importantly deepens your relationship with the student and provides them with an opportunity to be accountable for their actions. (You can find a restorative script at www.teacherrenewed.com).

We must honor the trust our students' families have put in us

As educators, our students are gifted to us. For

approximately one year, we are responsible for their livelihood and success. Too often I have seen educators work in isolation from families and even their students. Jay's family entrusted me to teach him, to treat him thoughtfully and fairly, and to provide him a safe environment. I let them down.

Students often have someone behind them who loves them. We have to show them this same love and keep working on ourselves to ensure our students have a safe and trusting environment to thrive in. Rita Pearson says, "Every child deserves a champion – **an adult who will never give up on them**, who understands the power of connection, and insists that they become the best that they can possibly be." More often than not, that champion is a member of the students' family but sometimes they are not. In those cases, we as educators have even more work to do, a responsibility to step into that champion role. I would say our aim should be to be champions for ALL of our students.

CHAPTER 3

Seeing Students as Their Family Sees Them

In my final year in the classroom, I had little to no patience, especially for a number of my male students. One of those students was Matt. While he got along with most students and teachers, he and I had a very contentious relationship. If I zagged, he zigged. He had a quick comment for everything. When his head was down, if I said, "listen" he would say, "I am." If I asked him to sit up, he would sit up but either keep his eyes closed or keep his arms folded as they were on the desk, still covering his face. Out of exhaustion, and not wanting to claim defeat, I would yell, have him leave class, or isolate him so he could not have an audience. My fuse was short with Matt so it didn't take much for me to lose my temper.

In one seemingly defiant instance, I decided to separate

Matt from his peers. I made him eat lunch in my classroom and, during the last portion of the day, required him to miss his classes and stay in my room with me. Being alone during lunch did not go over well with Matt's mom. She reached out to share not only her concern about my punitive consequences but also my lack of a relationship with Matt. She wrote me the following letter:

Ms. Adams,

I really need to speak to you about the time frame in which Matt was in the classroom by himself yesterday 12/15/2008. I really think something needs to be done as far as his strange behavior is concerned but the times that you had him stay in the room was utterly ridiculous!!!! I believe in the philosophy of [the school] but you on the other hand are clearly having issues with Matt that seem to fall under a dictatorship process. **I have told Matt over and over, if you do not like Ms Adams, I can't make you like anyone but you have to respect her. I feel the same thing applies here for you. If you do not care for Matt, WHICH IS FINE, I feel like you should at least respect him a little bit more than you have in the past.**

I understand your frustration. I really do. Hear me out and picture this scenario. For **supervision purposes** what if a fire broke out in the building that no one was in except Matt? What would you say to me and his father if he was severely injured? "He wasn't listening to me so he got hurt"? His life isn't a realistic consequence. You need to pick and choose your battles wisely. That wasn't a safe choice in my eyes. I don't want Matt in a class by himself for the substantial portion of his day. He missed two other classes; this is not acceptable. If he gets homework detention for work he doesn't understand then I have to figure out who picks him up. I have the contract that I signed as far as the discipline piece goes. We have to come up with a strategy that suits the unwanted behavior. We can take it back to behavior modification days. Do you ever compliment him when he is doing something positive or do you concentrate on the negative that leads to a non-resilient day? No one wants to be knocked down and then stepped on all at the same time. Matt tells me everything good or bad so I'm going to know what is going on. I don't want him in a room by himself, ever.

[The school's philosophy] states that teachers go above and beyond the regular school system. I feel that Matt knows what he has to do in order to be successful in the school; however, he is reluctant to come to your class because you approach him with a confrontational attitude. By no means is Matt an angel but it seems as though he has the most trouble in your class. I feel like there are other means of getting into his head. We need to focus on long-term scenarios rather than short-term excursions that aren't working. Please do not send another child to bring him his lunch. This is not a detention center. It is a school. You are beginning to hurt my feelings with these tactics and I am frustrated how no other teacher calls me to give me [negative feedback] or sits him in a room by himself [to a point where he] misses his other classes. They are just as valid as math is. I will see you around 6:00

but I needed to let you know how I feel before I got up to the school.

Thank you...

Matt's Mom

My Letter

Matt,

It has been some time. I have recently begun writing letters to my former students and felt a strong pull to reach out to you. I actually have a letter your mom wrote to me in December of 2008 that I reflect on periodically and share with other teachers to demonstrate how "well-intentioned" actions are not necessarily well intentioned. I have racked my brain to remember if I was ever able to reconcile my relationship with you and your mom and, given the distance, my guess is I never did. For this I am so sorry. While it has now been over a decade, please know that everything I am about to share is sincere and wish with all of my heart that I had shared these things with you while I was your teacher.

I remember how hard working you were. Your homework was pristine and meticulous. You came to math with your homework not just done but well done. You applied yourself to your learning and did a really outstanding job.

I remember how helpful you were. I saw this from afar, particularly with Mr. Pomis who had you help out with various things in his classroom, sending you on errands and trusting you as the good human you were and I am sure still are. Had I entrusted you in this same way, what a different experience you would have had not only in my classroom but likely at the school.

I remember your mom advocating and loving you with all of her heart and ensuring she had all sides of the story. I also think about the courage she had to write that letter to me. In it she acknowledged so much and even took responsibility in places she likely did not need to because it was me who was failing you in far too many ways.

You were a leader and had this way of influencing other students. If only I had seen this as leadership and embraced it, perhaps our relationship and your time at the school would have been different.

I hope things are going well for you and your family. Please share this letter with your mom as it is as much an apology to her as it is to you. Since leaving the school in 2009, I have been coaching teachers and I share the letter your mom wrote to me. No parent should ever have to write a letter like the one your mom had to write to me. I should have been better to you, Matt. You deserved it. Every day I reflect on my experience with you and your mom and commit to being better to my students.

Thank you for your lessons, your hard work, your leadership, and service.

Humbly,
Ms. Adams

Lessons and Resources

See the good in your students

Students tend to start each day anew but as adults we often hold onto the moments where students "did wrong." Our students have amazing, untapped potential. When we up the ante of expectation we must ground it in that special niche each student brings. Make a list of all the things you know a student is capable of. If there is something that might get on your nerves, turn it into something positive. Matt was a leader but I never let him lead. He was willing to do service but, instead, he served detention.

Be ready to repair your relationships

In order to see the good in students, it is imperative to have some nice one-on-one time with them. Let them know you want to repair what you have done and where you have gone wrong. Ask them how they feel about you. Encourage them to be honest. Let them tell you as much as they can about what they need and are looking for and then let them know you are going to work to do better. Let them know you will meet them half way and ask them if they are willing to meet you. Keep in mind, some students aren't always willing/able to meet you halfway. As an adult, you might in fact have to meet them 90% of the way first. Your happiness in the school year depends on the effort you are willing to put in. (You can find a restorative script at www.teacherrenewed.com).

If you aren't ready for this conversation I recommend you visit a class where the student you are struggling with is doing well. See how that teacher interacts with that student. Ask that teacher to list all of the things they love about the student.

When inclined to lecture, stop and listen

Too often, my interactions with Matt would leave me so frustrated my default was to lecture him on how to be a student, how he wasn't meeting the bar, how he needed to change his attitude, his behavior, etc. I would drone on and on making sure he heard everything he needed to hear. In reality, why would he even want to listen? I recall my parents yelling at me and rarely did I hear a single thing they said as I would just drown them out. Had I sat down and listened to Matt, asked him questions to understand why he behaved certain ways in my class, perhaps that would have changed some things between us. (Visit www.teacherrenewed.com where you can find a resource with helpful sentence stems to support you through this listening practice.)

CHAPTER 4

Giving Up

Every teacher has that one student, that student they wish they had been better for. While I have many students from my past I want to have done better for (heck, I am writing a book dedicated to them), I would say Jason is my "one student" I really never did enough (perhaps anything) for. For that I have the greatest regret. While for so many of the students I taught, I was able to reconcile the relationship, I was never able to with Jason.

I know Jason's grandmother was raising him but don't know much beyond that. He had learning challenges and therefore was part of our reading and math interventions. He was uninspired by the nature of fifth-grade fun and cuteness and rarely partook in celebratory chants, hugs, and games.

Jason was often considered insubordinate and noncompliant and would "act out," which resulted in not just a reaction from me but from all of the teachers on our staff. To gain the attention of his peers, often with a teacher's back turned, he would stick out his tongue or make silly faces, which would make other students smile and laugh. He would make chirping noises under his breath to see if a teacher would notice and sometimes would even manage to get other students to make similar noises for a whack-a-mole effect. These little things were not unique to my class, and eventually Jason was isolated in a room across the hall from my classroom.

There are quite a few stories that come to mind when reflecting back on my time as Jason's teacher but two stand out in particular.

The first was toward the beginning of the year when Jason was supposed to sit in an area of our cafeteria reserved for students who would not be dismissed with their peers in order to serve after-school detention. That day, I happened to be the only teacher in the room with the majority of our 90 fifth graders. Out of spite, or maybe it was opportunity or rebellion, Jason decided to stand up, run the length of the room, run back to his chair, and make one of his notorious noises. He smiled, students laughed, and my temper flared.

"You have got to be kidding! Sit down now and get yourself together!"

"Nah!" I remember Jason responding.

Laughter resonated through the cafeteria. I texted for back up. When my principal arrived, I brought Jason into my classroom. I called his grandma and let her know Jason could be picked up when he apologized to me. She said, "okay."

As Jason and I sat there, I tried lecturing him. "You won't act like that, you know what happens to kids who aren't successful in school." I tried bargaining, "You can go home as soon as you apologize." Power was my ultimate strategy.

Jason was a Black boy being forced to sit in the presence of a white female teacher whose pride had been injured. And he was being lectured about what society thinks about children who don't take their education seriously. Jason looked around the room and out the window but never at me. He rolled his eyes and played with his fingers. It was clear my "lecture" was not landing as intended, yet I droned on. I eventually got my "apology" and he went on his way. But things did not get better.

The next incident was around the middle of the year. Things were going pretty well in my math class and that particular day we were doing a fluency marathon where students worked the entire 90 minutes on drills to support their fluency in fractions. This marathon was called a "Fraction Frenzy." The activity was actually really joyful as we would tally every time a student completed an answer correctly. Classes would compete and by the end of the day we had thousands of tallies signifying really great fluency work.

At the start of the time I also "gifted" students with background music. The classes had made playlists and they would complete math problems to the beat of their favorite music. (Two of their favorites were Nas's "I Know I Can" and "Rubberband Man" by the Spinners.)

We had just started our frenzy and students were jovial, getting straight to work; calculating, checking, tallying, heads bobbing. This happened to be a day I was being observed by my principal and also happened to be the class Jason was in. Jason, like his peers, was enjoying the music but, instead of working, stood up and started dancing.

These days were typically some of the happiest in our classrooms and I wasn't about to have someone ruin things.

"Jason! Thanks to you, the class has lost their music!" I exclaimed.

Jason smiled, the class moaned, and the principal, who was observing, asked Jason to step out and pulled me to the side. He also had me keep the music on.

"If anyone else had stood up and danced, what would you have done?" the principal asked.

"I guess it would depend on who was dancing," I responded.

"Why would it depend?"

I thought for a second. "It would depend on whether they're dancing in order to disrupt the learning of other students."

"What would you have done if it was a student who is usually on point?"

"I would have gone to them and said, 'I can tell you are enjoying the music, but you also need to be working.'"

"Why couldn't you say that to Jason?" he asked.

Umph... touché.

I went out into the hallway and apologized to Jason. I then asked him if he thought the music would help him complete the problems or if it would be a distraction. He said he liked it. I asked if he felt he could continue working without distracting his learning and the class. He said "sure." And he did.

At the time, I had not considered what my words and actions would mean to Jason. All that occurred to me was that I was his teacher and he should be listening to me. I thought, "given the things I do for him and kids like him, they should be treating me with more respect." Yet, what respect did I show Jason? None.

Jason was suspended multiple times throughout the year

and spent two weeks in what we considered "isolation," where he was tutored, food was brought to him, and he had scheduled bathroom breaks. My interactions with Jason, even the words I use in this chapter, reflect a clear bias. "Called for backup," "serving detention," "isolation room," "power was my strategy." These are all phrases associated with policing, punishment, and penal institutions. These were also all phrases that came out of my mouth while interacting with Jason. I wasn't aware at the time that I was treating Jason like a criminal.

Jason came back to the school for a short amount of time the following school year, retained as a fifth grader. That was the last time I saw Jason. Over a decade later, I have come to learn Jason was arrested in 2018 and is serving four years in prison for battery.

My Letter

Jason,

I have looked you up on Facebook and other social media platforms many times over the years to see what you are up to. I was also trying to conjure up the courage to reach out with this letter and apologize. I finally found you. Sadly in the very place I hoped you would never end up.

I can't help but wonder what would be different for you if I had taken the time to know you, to trust you, to care for you the way all students deserve.

Jason, you have taught me that bias is deep and pervasive and I was perpetuating so many social constructs that reflected policing and incarceration tactics and not what education should ever be.

You taught me every student deserves a chance and that wrap-around services are critical for our students' long-term support. What would have been different in that time and space had our team not just focused on the punitive behaviors but, instead, created an environment where you felt supported and loved? What would have happened if we as a school team had brought in mental health supports you may have benefited from?

You taught me no person should be made to apologize. When things are an accident, I get it, but for you to apologize to me for my pride being injured is not okay. Today, I ask students if they want to apologize and if they say "yes," I first ask them why before they apologize to their peers or me.

Jason, I hope this letter makes it to you and you know how deeply sorry I am. No one is making me apologize. I know that I need to and I know you deserve it. I don't expect forgiveness, but I do assure and commit to you and all of my students now and into the future that they will be treated with love and care and I will do everything in my power to know them deeply.

Regretfully,

Ms. Adams

Lessons and Resources

Take a good look at your discipline policies

While our school adopted its policies from the network the school was affiliated with, we had liberty to adjust them as we saw fit. Nonetheless, I don't believe we did and, in too many circumstances, we perpetuated the school-to-prison pipeline. As you reflect on your discipline policies, I like to recommend Learning For Justice's *Code of Conduct: A Guide to Responsive Discipline* as a great starting place. It is imperative these analyses happen in all schools but especially schools where the majority of students come from marginalized communities.

Be mindful of the practices and even language you use when a student is not meeting expectations

Instead of requiring students to go to "detention," or be "isolated," it is okay to say instead "let's take some time to re-center." Instead of demanding that a student sit in an isolated room, it is okay to see if they need to pace it out, take a walk. Let them talk when they are ready. You would think that with practice, the adults in schools would improve and get creative in dealing with discipline. Instead, we seem to rely on coercion and compliance, resorting to clamping down, increasing our control, and pulling in the reins. This is how we know the "system" to exist, however more and more schools are reorienting their practices, working to dismantle an oppressive system. Be sure to take advantage of the many organizations out there whose work is truly providing a more just and equitable education system. The school in which I taught Jason, has made great strides and it is powerful to consider what they are doing for thousands of students across the country.

Apologies should never be coerced

I realize there are varying viewpoints here but one article synthesizing various studies explains: "it seems important to refrain from pushing one's child to apologize when he or she is not ready, or is simply not remorseful. Most young children don't view coerced apologies as effective." Take Jason for instance. He was not remorseful. I would argue, forcing him to apologize to me created an even greater rift in our relationship. If you have wronged a student and knowingly did, I believe it is imperative for educators to be vulnerable and apologize in order to help mend the relationship. In fact, for learning and transformation to happen, relationships are key. When students know us, their teachers, as we know them, our apologies mean something to them. If we believe our students owe an apology, they are much more likely to do so on their own when the apology is owed to someone they have a pre-existing relationship with. Had I had a relationship with Jason, I likely would not have felt the need to coerce an apology. There are a number of other things I could have done, including having a restorative conversation. Had I had a productive restorative conversation as a form of support, how different would my connections with students have been, especially with Jason?

CHAPTER 5

If I Had Done More, What Could Have Been Different?

Take a moment and picture a child, if you can, maybe an eleven year old with a gleaming smile that melts your heart. Their eyes light up as their smile widens and true joy sparkles across their face. Rarely does the smile subside because that child is just genuinely happy. Can you picture them? I can! The name of the child I'm picturing is Sean. While this is how I remember him, there were times I emotionally wiped that smile off his face.

Sean had a learning disability and received SPED services to support his learning. While learning was a challenge for him, making friends was not. Sean was a student everyone enjoyed being around. He could make anyone laugh. This was especially true when Sean was confronted with challenging work. He had a way of drawing attention to himself, riling up his peers and causing the class to erupt in explosive laughter. It was a great ploy.

While the students loved Sean's jovial side, when it disrupted classroom learning time, teachers would get frustrated, especially me. I often felt I had emptied my toolbox when it came to trying various strategies to keep Sean engaged and learning versus off task and bringing the class with him. Finally, one day, I had had enough and put his desk in my classroom's closet. It was large enough to use as a small office but, in essence, it was a closet.

I recall my principal bringing the superintendent of the county's public school system on a tour one of the days I had Sean in the "office" and the principal asking, "How do you expect me to explain to guests why we have a student sitting in a closet?"

I didn't have a good answer. I moved the desk to the corner of the room but still kept Sean isolated.

In the cafeteria during breakfast, lunch, and study hall, Sean was also typically isolated. He would sit at a solo desk on the outskirts of the rest of the tables, where his classmates would eat, talk, and work in community. Sean would raise his hand and get out of his seat incessantly asking for help. In return, I (along with my colleagues) would deduct money from his paycheck (our school's incentive system) and yell at him to go back to his seat. We would then put other students first who had their hand raised and who "knew" how to follow directions.

Over time, I found myself less and less drawn to his smile and more and more impatient with his lack of following rules, trying to be the class clown, and avoiding his work. In fact, the paycheck data showed I was the teacher who deducted the most from Sean's weekly paycheck. If it hadn't been for the deductions in my class or my presence, he would have likely made it to sit with the rest of the students in the cafeteria.

I never noticed this, so Sean's mom brought it to my attention. Similar to Matt's, Sean's mom was ready to confront my unconscious biases because what was blind to me was clear to her.

Sean's mom, however, took a different approach. Instead of writing an email, she wanted a meeting. In this meeting she shared that she recognized Sean's needs, his impulsivity, his desire to be liked, and also his ability to be magnetic, which was a strength but often distracted him and others from learning. She also brought up that he was just a boy. In fact, he was a young fifth grader. She reminded me there was a reason he had an IEP and that, as his teacher, I was bound to support his learning needs. She also shared that she was working with a doctor and psychologist to support what had recently been diagnosed as ADHD. He was preparing to start taking medication in the near future. She wasn't sure if that would be what he needed but all she wanted was for Sean to be successful. She wanted him to love school as much as he loved life. And, she wanted to be sure his teachers, especially me, provided him a space to love school.

While she did not bring up race, I do remember her saying to me, "I just want you to think first about how you respond to him, just as you want him to think first before he acts."

This was a life-changing conversation because it triggered in me a constant reminder. Sean's mom's voice was in my head not only when I responded to Sean's misbehavior but also when I responded to others'.

There is a reason, however, this story happens to be in part one of this book. While Sean matured and improved overtime, including the remainder of the time I had him as a student, and while his zest for school and learning grew, his life was cut short. At the mere age of 20 Sean's life ended at the hands of gun violence.

Since receiving this news, I have reflected on how my time with Sean could have been different. Instead of putting him in a closet I wish I had put him on a trajectory where he would still be alive and thriving today.

My Letter

Dear Sean's Mom,

I am deeply saddened writing you this letter. Mr. Pomis advised that I not write the letter given the circumstances of Sean's life and so if you don't want to read this I understand.

You see, these last few years I have set out to write letters to students I know I could have been a better teacher to and Sean was definitely one of them.

He lit up a room and provided so much joyous energy anywhere he went. Students loved him and, even though he got in trouble in class, I can say there wasn't a teacher who didn't have a special place in their heart for Sean.

I loved returning to the school and seeing how he was maturing. He always greeted me with a big beautiful smile, despite how I treated him as his teacher.

Sean taught me that we as educators need to see our students' future selves. Every day we should invest in what we want for them and what they want for themselves. We have to remember the time we get with them is precious and, while a small mark on their timeline in life, we can make a huge impact, for better or worse. We have to make it count.

He taught me that, as students bring joy to school, we as educators must channel and embrace that joy, not try to take it away. Sean had fun, he loved to play and make people happy.

Had I been patient, accepted him for who he was, and used other tactics to channel his joy in the classroom instead of suppress it, how different would our relationship have been. And, while I remember him growing, I also know that had I done more for him and let him be who he was, his growth could have been even more profound.

Sean taught me that an education is not a bulletproof vest and what we provide our students and how we work with them to support their lives when they are outside of school is also critical. While me being a better teacher for Sean during the year I had him in my class may not have changed the trajectory of his life, I could have at least celebrated his rare and unwavering joy and the bright light that he was.

My heart is with you,

Kelley

Lessons and Resources

Meet Students where they are both academically and behaviorally

I knew Sean had significant academic needs as well as behavioral needs and yet I focused more on holding him to our school's vision and policies. While I am not advocating lowering the bar, I do realize this was a mistake. He was not ready to meet me halfway and I disciplined him for that. I needed to provide 90% of the support and let him meet me 10% of the way. Looking back, and having now met thousands of students, I understand that, while Sean was not necessarily "acting his age" due to factors in his life, his actions reflected where he was emotionally. A school counselor recently told me students impacted by trauma often have the emotional maturity of a student half their age. This was profound and made me think of Sean. If that is true then Sean would have had the emotional maturity of a five- or six-year-old boy. As I reflect on this, and consider boys' behaviors in that age range, Sean's actions make more sense to me. I thought I could discipline him into maturity, which was not a healthy tactic. If you have a student who has great academic and emotional/behavioral needs I highly recommend considering the child's background and how it impacts their behaviors. Support their needs instead of disciplining them. As I mentioned in the years following, I would visit the school where I taught Sean and I could see his evolving maturity. After I left, the school transformed the SPED program in a way that was much more receptive to the needs of students who receive SPED services and the results were palpable.

Imagine your students 10 to 20 years out

Each year I was focused on where my students needed to be at the end of the year. What I didn't realize was how limiting this was. I needed to have more robust visions for my students and work backward from there. Most years I did some form of interest survey that included asking what students wanted to be when they grew up. If I had actually used this to inform my interactions then I would have likely changed the life trajectory of so many students. If I had treated my students like doctors, professional athletes, moms and dads, their experiences in my classroom would have been markedly different. Each year as you get a new set of students I recommend taking into consideration who they want to be, both professionally and as human beings, and then treat them accordingly, helping them nurture and develop the skills they will need to grow into the adults they dream of becoming.

Humbling Moments but Transformative Outcomes

CHAPTER 6

Not Giving Up

Did you know current statistics show new teachers leave the profession, at rates of somewhere between 10% and 15% over their first five years of teaching? (NCSC, 2014) While my first year was one of the most challenging of my life, my third year was equally if not more challenging and had me thinking about becoming part of the aforementioned statistic.

After two years of teaching middle school students with Special Needs in Rocky Mount, NC, I decided to move to Charlotte, NC with Aaron (my now husband). This was a fresh start for me. Not only was I moving, I also felt I could follow my dream of becoming an elementary school teacher.

I found a 4th/5th grade teaching position at a local charter school that followed various pedagogical philosophies. The principles on which the school was founded included:

constructivist learning and emergent curriculum through the Emilia Reggio framework along with arts integration. Further, we were a community-based school, which meant we also worked in close partnership with various community programs, schools, universities, and nonprofits. The school catered to a diverse array of children with approximately 75% of students qualifying for free or reduced lunch and about 65% being students of color.

The school expected all third, fourth, and fifth grade teachers to uphold the model framework of the school and follow the North Carolina State Standards given that students in those grades would have to take the NC End of Grade (EOG) reading and math tests. It is also important to mention, I received the job one week before the school year began, meaning I had a lot to learn in very little time.

On the first family night of the year (which took place three days after my start date) one of the kindergarten/first grade teachers exclaimed, "Wow you have some big kids! I hope you are ready for it." I remember my heart beating a bit faster but thinking, "I've got this. After two years of teaching in a middle school as well as teaching students with various special needs, I can do anything. Teaching in a general education classroom with 26 students will be a breeze." Little did I know, my two years of experience was not enough.

Following the first day of the school year during my first year of teaching I had written in my journal: "Today was my first day ever teaching. It was eerily calm." The second year I wrote: "Similar to last year, my first day was once again, eerily calm. Maybe the first day of school is just like this." My first day at this new school, however, was anything but calm. That evening I wrote in my journal: "Today was pure chaos! Tomorrow has to be better."

Because this was an elementary school I came in believing students would be eager to learn, bright eyed, easily managed, and obedient. My class, while consisting of some bright-eyed and eager students, also consisted of students who had a lot more experience at the school than me. Some had been there since kindergarten and had been each other's classmates for five years. They already knew how to push each other's buttons, and they quickly shared (some even demanded) who they could and could not sit by. Being the only 4th/5th grade teacher, I also had three sets of siblings making up nearly 25% of the class. Additionally, like many classrooms this day and age, I had three students who were diagnosed with ADHD and prescribed medication. (Note: I say "prescribed" because they did not always take their medication.)

Because we were a small school, I taught a full day. I ate lunch with and even took my students to recess. Since the school was located in a church in downtown Charlotte, we walked each day to a park approximately a quarter of a mile away for recess. This meant I spent a good portion of the day walking 26 students through the city.

By the end of that first week, I was already questioning if I was cut out for teaching. I was not ready for some of the students' emotional needs. Siblings were distracted by siblings. Emotional outbursts were a norm for a few students. Plus, I had done little to build culture among the class, mistakenly thinking expectations, management, and keeping students "in check" was all I needed to do.

By the second week of school, Anissa Miller (a dream of a partner teacher who saved my life many times), offered to take three students off my hands, two of whom were from sibling pairs and another whom she had taught the year before. This not only put her class at over 20 students that year but also made her class a combined 2nd/3rd/4th grade class. If she thought ill or negatively of it, she never showed it. She was there to support students, their families, and her colleagues. While this was immeasurably helpful, the already challenging dynamics in my class continued.

At the three-week mark, I revamped my behavior system but, alas, behaviors didn't change. Except for mine. I had taken to yelling. Five students in particular tested my will and patience every day: Q, Kira, Allen, Alton, and Tre. Rarely did these five students do the work I assigned them. If something did not go their way they would erupt into temper tantrums and yelling. Four of the five were at or above grade level academically (similar to Jay), however, their emotional and maturational needs were, at that time, beyond my ability to handle with my teacher toolbox. All five grew bored quickly and, when redirected, would protest by interrupting my instruction, laying on the floor crying loudly and often refusing to do their work. Not surprisingly, other students would become frustrated and their frustration only added to the outbursts of the five.

While I had taught students with behavioral and emotional disabilities in my first year of teaching, I guess I didn't feel the strategies I used in that classroom, which had helped my students progress, applied here. The more I tried to "manage," the more students acted out, and the more they acted out, the more I yelled. I even took to isolating the five students. They were seated with their backs to the rest of the class and were only allowed to be at the end of the line. Their isolated yet collective dynamic only made matters worse. And I kept yelling.

By October, in my heart, I was done with teaching. I couldn't do it anymore. I thought teaching elementary students was my dream but it so clearly wasn't. At one point the school leader called me into his office and told me the offices above us were complaining about my yelling.

Even more embarrassingly, my yelling was caught on television. On one of our days visiting downtown we were walking back to the school and took a detour. The students noticed the afternoon news was being broadcast via one of the buildings (imagine the Today Show patrons standing in the background smiling and waving). The students embraced the opportunity to be in the background of a television program and began shouting with glee, waving excitedly and jumping up and down. While they were overjoyed, I was annoyed and embarrassed and, well, yelled. The next day one of the local college students who happened to be volunteering in my classroom that day said her mom had been watching the news and wondered, "who's this white lady yelling and losing her mind?" Not my proudest moment.

Shortly following the news incident, family teacher conferences came, which were not only humbling but also a pretty desperate wake-up call. Families were threatening to take their children out of the school as many expressed to me and the school leader that this was not the school they signed up for.

The most humbling conference was with a mom who had two students at the school and had been there a lot longer than me. Always dressed to the nines in her business outfits and heels, she carried herself with ease and confidence. She had a deep voice and never shied away from speaking her truth. I was equal parts in awe and intimated by this mom. Her words will forever be imprinted in my mind, "If you don't want to teach my children then you need to leave. Yelling is not teaching. But know this, if you stay, I will help you! You NEED help and we are a community. Make up your mind." I took her up on the support and decided I would give it another go.

The week following the conferences I took two mental health days. I spent both days restructuring my classroom. In my planning, I was committed to calling on the families to help and I was going to make this work. First, I reset my classroom approach. This time I implemented a stamp system called Operation S.M.A.R.T (Scholarly, Motivated, Accountable, Respectful, and Think). The focus would be on the positives and celebrating when my students were doing well instead of focusing on what they weren't doing. This new system would allow students to show up as leaders and the premise would be to help cultivate a community.

While the classroom system and perspective was a shift, the biggest change I made was how I worked alongside my students' families. One evening I invited all of my students' parents and guardians to my apartment complex for a barbecue. This was the ultimate game changer. Aaron grilled hamburgers and hotdogs and we broke bread on a rooftop terrace overlooking the city. Families got to know me better but, more importantly, I got to know them.

Within a month, families were volunteering in my classroom, bringing in snacks and supporting our efforts.

In the coming months, the entire dynamic of the classroom began to change. Through a community partnership with a local private school, students began researching colleges and talking about their dream universities. We partnered with Johnson C. Smith University, a local Historically Black University, that provided science lessons and support. Each year students and a professor would come to our school and focus on a scientific theme. That year's theme was biology with an emphasis on photosynthesis. Culminating the eight-week program, the class was required to present on what they learned in an artistic way. The students decided they wanted to put on a play so we wrote a "play." It was a mere 20 minutes with students explaining, through drama and song, the concept of photosynthesis.

We also hosted a coffee house poetry slam. One of my student's family members worked at Dean and Deluca's Coffee shop and had the store donate coffee and treats. Another worked at Chick-fil-A and had their job donate catered nuggets and sandwiches. Another family donated a brand new flat screen TV to be raffled off so we could raise money for the annual 4th/5th grade field trip. We raised enough money to visit Wake Forest along with other historical places in the area. We even managed to raise enough money to celebrate the 5th grade culmination with a limousine ride for all twelve fifth graders along with a fancy lunch with their families at a local restaurant in downtown Charlotte.

We had so many qualitative, monumental and historical successes worth celebrating. While the school did not necessarily put too much emphasis on EOG's given its values, we were still required to take the state test. One hundred percent of my fifth graders and 90% of my fourth graders passed both the math and reading tests that year.

My Letter

Dear Graduating Classes of 2012 and 2013,

I was ready to quit teaching all together that year. For as long as I can remember, my dream was to be an elementary-school teacher but early in that school year, I figured I would go be a barista at Starbucks because surely that had to be easier.

Thankfully, you and your families did not give up on me. Your families rallied and supported me because of their love for you and all of the students in that class.

You all taught me expectations and "management" are not enough to support a successful classroom and that re-lationships lie at the heart of any successful classroom. Even though many of you already knew each other, you made me realize how important it is to build a classroom culture where the teachers and students know one another deeply and the teacher understands and knows their students' families.

You all taught me just because a school has a "Low Income" title does not mean a school has little. That year I learned wealth and riches come in many different forms. The greatest form is love for children. While some families might not have had monetary means, they had many, perhaps more important, resources. When you as students asked for some-thing for the class, it was ours. From a T.V. being donated to always having ample classroom snacks, to providing a genuine coffee house, and so much more, the families rallied together and gave this group of 4th and 5th graders so much.

You all taught me humility in the most humble of ways. I came in cocky, once again thinking I alone had all the answers. As people reached out their hands to me and I took them, I learned I could hang on a lot longer. I could keep teaching. Did I master the art of teaching and relationships that year? Absolutely not. I did, however, learn this is not isolated work. The old adage "it takes a village" couldn't be better applied to the lessons you all taught me.

I miss you all and appreciate the memories. I know in too many ways, especially early on, I did you wrong but, thanks to your families, your biggest advocates, the year turned out alright.

Thank you for your bright-eyed, eager selves.

With All My Heart,

Ms. Adams

Lessons and Resources

Culture is key
You have likely heard the quote "Culture eats strategy for lunch." In that first year of teaching elementary school, I found this to be completely true. When I revamped my

classroom, prioritizing building a healthy and supportive culture, the dynamic changed. When you need to reset your classroom, or if you are new to teaching, begin with your vision. What do you want to be true for your students by the end of the year? What will your students be able to know and do? Who do you want your students to become beyond your classroom and in life? Now, take that statement, parse it out and decide how you will help your students get there. These are not lessons in isolation, but recurring themes, practices, exercises, discussions that happen throughout the year. The first week I introduced Operation S.M.A.R.T, we spent a day on each characteristic, writing, reading, discussing, and reflecting. We said a daily pledge calling out actions students would take for each word and students would write daily, weekly, and quarterly goals prompted by the S.M.A.R.T. acronym. This intentionality around culture is key to your students' success.

Lean on your students' families

You are not alone in this work. I don't know if I had a savior complex, if I was just naive, or had something to prove, but the second I surrendered my pride and asked for help (well, a parent more so demanded I ask for help… thank you Ms. Toshiko) my whole experience changed. I was happier, my students were happier, and their families were happier. Not only did I set aside my pride but I was also forced to look at my biases and the stereotypes I was holding onto. Our students' families are generally their students' greatest advocates. Advocacy shows up in very different ways. Just as educators must see the gifts and potential of our students, we have to do the same for their families. When you do, students and families see you differently. You form a bond of trust with them and when that happens so much more is possible for our students.

In the event you as an educator encounter less supportive families (and, sadly, you will) you, the teachers, will likely need to be those students' biggest advocates. And if for whatever reason you can't be, it is imperative to find an adult in those students' lives who they can trust. Whether a counselor, the school receptionist, health tech, administration, or faculty in a mentorship program, as members of the educational community, we can all help ensure all students have advocates, an "extended family," that will support their development and well-being.

Be humble

As a white female educator who has taught primarily students of color, I can only imagine what my students' families thought of me. Actually, I know because some of them told me (and I thank them for that now). I was a cocky young white girl from Colorado who had taught for two years and thought I knew so much. What I found out in that third year was that I knew nothing in comparison to what I had to learn. We can always learn, improve, and develop more and that year was a pivotal point in my learning journey. When you have a colleague like Annisa Miller, stop, watch, listen, and learn. When I did, I became a better teacher. When you have students' parents and family members like Wendy Vandehei, Toshiko Cunningham, Ann Betts, Josette, Betty Jones,

Christine and Kurtley Jones, Scott and Linda Keeter (I could go on...), you know you are set up for success. Find ways to know your students' families. Find ways to connect with them beyond family-teacher conferences and let them know you are going to love and care for their child as much as you possibly can.

CHAPTER 7

High Expectations

In writing letters to my former students and wanting to send them, I often had to go beyond Facebook and other social media platforms to see if I could even find them. There were times when I found former students who were in law school, had earned master's degrees, even had children of their own. So many things to celebrate! And then there were the not so great things.

As I searched for Neal, I found multiple arrest records and mugshots. This was not the reality I wanted for this sweet boy. Neal was a boy whose dyslexia was so severe that even as an eighth grader he could hardly write and still struggled with reading. Neal, however, was not an eighth grader when I was his teacher. He was in second grade.

That year I had requested to have a specific population of students in my classroom. I wanted all of the first and second grade students who were still performing below grade level. This was my first year teaching lower elementary and I wanted to prove how much growth I could realize.

Neal was one of my first picks. I knew he received SPED services for a learning disability. I also knew that, entering second grade, he was still reading and writing at a pre-kindergarten level, took medication for ADHD, and was impulsive.

More importantly, I knew he was a sweetheart who wanted friends. He loved video games, he gave the best hugs, and loved his mom and new baby sister with all his heart.

These positive attributes were what got Neal and me through our share of challenges as the year went.

Most days, Neal came to school late. I am not sure if this was due to his mom having difficulty waking up or if Neal was the one who struggled in the morning. What quickly became clear to me was that the day could go one of two ways depending on how Neal's hair looked. On days his hair was in tight braids, I knew we were in for a great day. On days when his hair was unkempt, it meant there was likely a struggle ahead. Regardless of how the day *could* go, I was committed to ensuring Neal walked into a peaceful, loving, and consistent classroom.

One day when Neal came into class looking a bit disheveled he didn't want to write or come to reading groups. I gave him space and said he could work on Thinkshop. While I worked with small groups, the rest of the class worked independently. Neal took a place in the corner of the classroom near a friend he liked to work with. When it was time to pull the friend into reading groups, however, Neal stayed in the corner. Upon the friend's return to the corner, he immediately came back to inform me of two things: (1) the friend was bleeding because Neal had poked him with a tack and (2) Neal had put tiny holes all over the wall with the tack.

I was livid at Neal. I revoked his ability to play at recess (instead he would have to do a reflection walk on the field) as well as the opportunity to sit next to his friend during Thinkshop.

At home that night I was sharing with Aaron how upset I was at Neal and how unbelievable his actions were. Aaron seemed surprised by my attitude. "Didn't you say Neal was impulsive? Why weren't you keeping an eye on him? How did he have a tack in the first place? A lot of time had to have passed for him to have made all of those holes, right?"

True to nature, I wanted to be defensive. Couldn't Aaron just take my side for once? I likely replied, "Yeah but..."

- I have other students in the class.
- He was in the corner being quiet... for once.
- I can't be expected to keep my eyes on him at all times.

In working through my defensiveness, I realized I actually

could have kept Neal from poking holes in the walls and his friend. While I couldn't control the kind of morning Neal had before entering the classroom, I could control what happened in my classroom.

From that point on, Neal was my sidekick in everything. He had a special desk next to my small group table that he would sit at so I could give him additional academic support. I differentiated his Thinkshop to give him some play breaks. He also had the opportunity to earn time sitting and working with peers of his choice as he got things done.

Coming to me on a kindergarten reading and first-grade math level that year, Neal left on a second-grade level in reading and math. In both core subjects, he had grown more than a grade level. While he did not end up at the third-grade level as I would have hoped him to be at by the end of that year, that moment of venting to Aaron provided me an opportunity to get rid of my "yeah but" and take on a "what's in my control?" attitude.

Now, I mentioned Neal being in eighth grade. When I left the classroom as a teacher in 2009 I supported and coached teachers throughout Charlotte. Over the course of three years, Neal was a student in two of my teachers' classrooms, once when he was in sixth grade and the other when he was in eighth grade.

In both classrooms, it was amazing to get to see this sweet, loving student have such extraordinary teachers and share in celebrating his caring demeanor and academic accomplishments.

Neal's later involvement with the criminal legal system is not a future I would wish for any of my students. Still, I am so glad I had the opportunity to have Neal in my classroom. He taught me so much and, while I have not found him to give him his letter, here it is all the same.

My Letter

Dear Neal,

I am not sure where you are but I write this letter to you through the universe, knowing that you had such a deep impact on my heart. Rarely were you on time for school but you always showed up.

From you I learned that, instead of vilifying you for your impulsivity, I needed to lean on my own creativity to support you. Did it mean we spent a lot more time together? Yes. But did it also mean I was ultimately able to help and support you along your educational journey? Absolutely. And that extra time together allowed me to develop a relationship with you that helped me hold you to a higher standard. You and I learned to trust one another and, in return, we had each other's backs. You worked hard in my class and you made so much progress.

Despite the learning challenges, you were so incredibly creative and when we tapped into your creativity you soared. I am not sure if you remember but before we had you writing stories on your own, you would first draw pictures. The pictures were vivid and detailed and video-game worthy. We would sit at the kidney table. You would share your drawing and I would write and write and write. Your stories were out-of-this-world creative and, as time went on, you began writing your own stories.

Do you recall the two times I "found" you? Once in sixth grade and the other in eighth? Both times you were at different schools and the teachers I was coaching both happened to be leading your SPED classes. I remember observing that first time in the charter school where students wore button ups, ties, and sweater vests. You came into the class and, unknowingly, I was sitting in your seat. I ended up staying for the entire class. I remember Ms. H saying, "Wow! Neal did so great today!" She had told me she knew you had potential but was really able to see it that day. You asked me to come visit you again and that year I did multiple times. Then, something similar happened when you were in eighth grade. That day in class, your teacher had you going to various centers around the classroom. I followed you, you worked, and I helped.

Man, I miss you. I wish my impact had had a lasting effect. I wish some of the behaviors you exhibited in my class lasted into your middle- and high-school years. I wish I had taught you to better advocate for what you need to ensure your long-term success.

I am glad for the time we had, I just wish I had done more.

Grateful and Regretful,
Ms. Adams

Lessons and Resources

Your locus of control is likely greater than you know
Situations like the ones I had with Neal are real for many teachers. Of course, we are likely not the root cause of why students behave the way they do, but when we expand our locus of control it is amazing how much of a positive influence we can have. In talking with Aaron that night and now 16 years later, I have realized there is a lot more in my control than I often think. It can be exhausting but the time I put into being with Neal, having him near me, getting in front of his impulsivity, not only made my classroom calmer, it supported Neal's behavior and also helped him grow academically and behaviorally.

When you have students who are causing issues in your classroom, it is imperative you take those students and ensure you have created boundaries and support systems all around them to help ensure they can be successful. Perhaps it is a special seat near you during all times of instruction. Perhaps it is giving them "jobs" that help quell their energy (e.g., errands to other teachers). The bottom-line is to ensure that not every response/approach is punitive and that you have an extended amount of control within your circle of power.

All students have strengths

Neal had a lot of challenges, between his dyslexia and ADHD, learning and the "typical" structure of school was not necessarily where he thrived. On the other hand, he was amazing at video games, his creativity was endless, and his energy when outside playing tag or sports with his friends was wonderful. We were able to use these avenues to support his success in school. We learned that graphic novels (large print) were great for him to read. He also loved books based on video games. We learned that when he could draw first and dictate to me his stories he was able to complete his work. I will also add that, while reading and writing weren't his academic "strengths," math was. He did an amazing job of making sense of numbers and oftentimes the logic behind mathematical problem solving was his niche. He loved riddles and having his brain challenged. Had I merely focused on his behaviors and the fact that he struggled so much with reading and writing, that year would have been a wash for him. Instead, I was incessant in finding what he could do and leveraging those things. What I found was he was a pretty amazing kid.

Find your students' strengths and leverage them like their life depends on it! In some cases, it might.

You can't always rely on medicine

This one is extraordinarily difficult and, even in my "veteran" years as a teacher, it was hard to think about. Medication was not guaranteed to work for all of my students who took it and the "off" days when they had not taken their medicine for whatever reason were so challenging. What I have come to realize is that we need to plan for who the student is and what they need without the medicine because those days will happen.

I knew that while one of the greatest consequences for students was to lose a part of their play time at recess and have to do a "walk-flection," the "off days" for Neal were the days he needed the play time more than anything. I therefore worked alongside my classroom family volunteers as well as our support staff to provide him with some morning time fun as soon as he got part of his morning work done. They would go outside and play for 10 minutes just to get some energy out. Neal would complete his work incrementally with an added "reward" at the end of that time so the amount of time he could focus was just right and he knew something special would be at the other end.

I have found this to be very helpful, especially now as a school administrator. Often for our students who need something more, I am the one our teachers are partnering with to support those individual needs that might deter our students from learning and/or distract their peers from their learning.

While we have students who take medicine, we have plans for the days when the medicine is not in their system. These days are typically easy to recognize.

Visit www.teacherenewed.com for ways you can support students on those off days!

CHAPTER 8

Students Want to be Loved

Brie had beautiful, bubbly handwriting and dotted her "i's" and wrote her periods with hearts. When she read, she read slowly, phonetically, and struggled with comprehending the text. Yet, she read. Words were often misspelled and she used little to no punctuation (except in the case of a heart period here and there, of course). Yet, she filled pages with her thoughts. Math seemed even more challenging for her as she would often leave problems unsolved. Yet, with help, she tried. It is hard to admit, but I went too long before recognizing and appreciating these "yet" moments.

For most of her life, Brie went back and forth between her mom and dad. At the time I met her as a fifth grader, she and her siblings were living with their dad and stepmother and her mom was in jail.

Various administrators and teachers who taught Brie's siblings told me about the unpredictable and, at times, unsafe home life the three children shared. I couldn't help but wonder why the state kept them in a house if they knew or had reason to believe the children were not safe. I later found out, however, keeping kids together was the top priority, and being with their biological mom or dad provided the only guarantee the siblings stayed together.

That school year, my class was a dual fourth/fifth grade class where the students' academic abilities ranged from kindergarten to ninth grade. I therefore did a lot of small-group teaching. To support these expansive and varying learning levels, I continued to use "Thinkshop," where students worked on different tasks and centers that supported their learning while I met with small groups throughout the day. During these small group times, depending on the Thinkshop task, Brie could be found doing one of a few things: rushing through the work to get it done; not doing the work at all and instead, doing odd things here and there (e.g., fluffing pillows, cleaning up tables, organizing the library); or talking to other students. In my mind, I saw this as her refusing to do her work, not taking her education seriously, and distracting her peers from their learning. That year, I implemented a "color system" where students' names were displayed on a wall with a pocket of paper colors. They would publicly turn their cards over depending on their behavior (blue being the best and red being the worst). Brie ended many days on the less "favored" colors, and consequences followed.

In the fall, I needed to be observed for one of my teacher certification classes, so I asked Aaron, who observed and coached teachers for a living, to observe me. He watched me teach. He even watched the transitions to and from the bathroom and recess. As my boyfriend, I just knew he wouldn't find fault in my teaching and would celebrate all of the great things I did. After all, I was differentiating like a beast, and that day, I provided students with an application assessment regarding translations for math. My reality, however, was just that, *my* reality. Aaron remained objective and productively critical. He gave me feedback, and I wish I accepted it with grace, love, and appreciation as the feedback and reflection would have improved my classroom tenfold. Instead, I was taken aback by his feedback. I became sensitive and defensive and made sure he knew how hard I worked and how much he didn't know about my classroom.

Aaron did point out strengths in different areas but the most critical feedback he gave me had little to do with the instruction and more with classroom culture and my reactions toward Brie. He noticed how I called her out when she wasn't in her seat or assigned area doing her work. The bomb came when he mentioned the moment I snapped at Brie while the class was transitioning from the bathroom back to the classroom.

When she stepped out of the line, I made it clear she would be turning her card upon our arrival back into the classroom. She opened her mouth to argue but I was not having it that day. I cut her off before she could say anything. "That's the consequence of getting out of line Brie. You know the expectation and I expect each of you to abide by it." I was offended that she dared to contend with my expectations, particularly when we were in the hallway where the head of school and office manager could hear and see us.

When Aaron brought this up, I blamed Brie. I jumped to explain how she was never doing what I expected her to do, how she was constantly "trying" to get other kids in trouble and off task because she had no regard for them, and how she *never* abided by my rules.

"Never?" He asked me.

"Yes! Never!" I replied.

He went on to ask me if I knew what Brie was doing when she stepped out of line. I don't remember my reply but I do remember what he said.

"She was trying to help someone in front of her because they had dropped something."

He explained that as he watched Brie, she at times was avoiding her work when she left her area, but she was often going to other students to ask for help. After all, I had a "three before me" rule where students had to ask three other students before coming to me for help. Whether someone helped Brie or couldn't, she typically stuck around to chat. In my eyes, this caused a distraction and showed a lack of regard for my classroom expectations. Yet, her "lack of regard" for my expectations was, more times than not, an effort to be helped, to help, and to connect.

At first, I didn't take Aaron's feedback to heart nor did I let up on Brie. Then, fortunately for myself and more importantly for Brie, we hit a turning point, one that opened my eyes and heart to Brie in a way that helped me really see her.

One day, on the way back to school from the downtown children's library, a woman approached Brie. We were mere steps away from the school.

Brie, being near the end of the line, yelled in panic, "Ms. Adams!"

Worried and confused, I stopped the class and approached Brie. I noticed she was stiff, wide eyed, and tight lipped as the woman kept trying to convince Brie to talk to her. I asked the woman if I could help her, and she explained she was Brie's mom. When I asked Brie if this was true, Brie nodded yes. It was my understanding Brie's mom had been in jail earlier in the school year but I wasn't sure if they were in communication or if her mom was even allowed to have contact with Brie. When I asked Brie if she was supposed to be in contact with her mom, she shook her head no.

I didn't know how to handle the situation. I was only three and a half years into my teaching career and had never encountered anything quite like this. We were close enough to the school that the class could sit on a lawn in front of the school building. I worried Brie's mom was not supposed to know where Brie and her siblings went to school so, instead of sending Brie into the building, I sent her to sit with her classmates.

While I spoke to Brie's mom, a few of Brie's peers took her by the shoulders and sat with their arms wrapped around her. I asked Brie's mom if there was someone I could get in touch with to confirm if Brie was allowed to talk to her. I also asked if she wanted me to call Brie's father to perhaps grant permission for Brie to talk with her. I didn't feel comfortable with them talking until then. It appeared Brie didn't want a conversation either.

Fortunately, Brie's mom left. As she walked away, the class and I all sat on the grass talking while I, along with a classmate, held Brie's hand and others rubbed her back. She cried and I remember her whispering, "I just want to be loved." Once her mom was out of sight, I led my class back into the school where we huddled together on the carpet, peers still cuddling with Brie, the rest listening to me read aloud our after-recess book and the class overflowing with love.

Brie felt this love, and it seemed everything in that moment turned around for her. No longer was there tension between us and my blame subsided. She trusted me, I trusted her. This trust turned into hard work and joy. She stopped avoiding work and continued asking for help from others. Her classmates gave it to her. Brie stayed after school with me almost daily and received tutoring. Brie finished the year at a fifth-grade reading level and fourth-grade math level.

She grew in academics but, more importantly, she grew in trust, love, leadership, and confidence.

My Letter

Dear Sweet Brie,

I don't know if you recall the conversation we had after that incident with your mom. When I checked in with you later that day, I remember you saying how tired you were and how much you just wanted to be loved. So much had been put on you in such a short lifetime and all you wanted was to be supported and successful. You gave so much of yourself to everyone each and every day and too often it was clear how little you had left to give yourself.

Perhaps you don't remember this either but in 2009, I found you! While coaching a teacher we were reviewing math papers and I came across what appeared to be your first name and last initial as both the dot in the "i" and period were made with hearts. I asked the teacher if this paper was yours. To my heart's happiness, it was. The next day, I visited you in that classroom, and we caught up. You shared all you had been through over the last four years and, despite spending a mere 15 years on this earth, the weight of the world remained on your shoulders.

Brie, you taught me so much in the short time I had the opportunity to be your teacher. I learned how much can be put on a child and that, when in the classroom, teachers can and must help alleviate that fear and anxiety by providing a safe and trauma-informed space for each of their students.

I learned that a "busy" student is not always avoiding work but rather working to connect and learn. As teachers, we must provide space and meaningful opportunities to ensure students who need space for connection have it. Teachers must ensure students are not punished for finding ways to do so, especially if the teacher hasn't offered that space for their students.

I learned that students often show how they want to be loved through their actions. What they project is often what they need. When others were given the opportunity to help you and provide for you, you learned so much more.

I wish it hadn't taken so long for me to learn these lessons. Thank you for providing me a lens into your heart and teaching me that all students can be loved and respected in their classrooms.

My Heart to Yours,
Ms. Adams

Lessons and Resources

Be mindful off foundational human needs

When students enter our classrooms having had traumatic life experiences, learning material is often the last thing on their minds, especially if their most basic life needs are not being met. Teachers are no longer "just teachers" but must lean into their role as educators. There is a difference between teaching and providing an education. No matter how you define teaching versus providing an education, our students are coming to us with histories and experiences many of us could never imagine. Especially if we are granted privileges due to our backgrounds and if our backgrounds do not reflect those of students from marginalized communities. When we take a step outside of mere classroom expectations and really think about the human lives in front of us, we can become true educators. While the work is beyond hard, what is amazing is when we provide a safe space for our students to connect. When we do this, more learning happens but there is also more joy and less obstacles for our classroom community. Consider how your classroom culture and routines can support some of those foundational needs.

Rid yourself of the potential "Deficit Ideology Detour"

In Gorski's "Avoiding Racial Equity Detours" (Gorski, 2019) he explains how we as educators, "[presume] we can resolve racial inequities by simply teaching students of color to have grit, [which] is like presuming we can resolve climate change by teaching coastal communities to swim faster." Our efforts as anti-racist and non-oppressive educators must focus on "eliminating conditions that marginalize students--never on fixing students of color." As I reflect on Brie's story, I can see how my classroom systems and expectations actually perpetuated harm and did little to recognize my students were not there to be fixed but to be loved, supported, and provided space to showcase all they bring to this world. We as educators can and must do this by incorporating culturally responsive practices within our classrooms and ensuring that we have done the self work to explore and understand how we might be operating with a "savior complex" or pressing upon our students a white dominant culture that does not allow our students to feel true liberation. (Visit www.teacher-renewed.com/resources for ways to create a more culturally responsive and liberatory classroom.)

Be observed

Don't be afraid of observation. Find someone who cares about and will be honest with you because they want you and your students to succeed. I thought asking Aaron to observe me would mean I would be off the hook, and he would only see all of the positive things I did. His honesty and time in my classroom that day, despite the fact it took me longer than it should have to understand what he had to say, was critical in my journey of becoming an anti-racist and non-oppressive educator. Try your best to remain open when the honesty comes. We owe this to our students.

CHAPTER 9

Caught and Taught

"How dare you speak to my child like that?! How dare you speak to anyone's child like that?!"

I turned around to see Ms. Frank. I had just finished reprimanding her daughter Nala, and making Nala leave tutoring because she had been talking in line.

Before I could say anything, Ms. Frank continued. She expressed how ridiculous the school's and my expectations were. She described how Nala, her daughter and a Black child, would come home and say she got in trouble even though she had done nothing wrong. Seeing it for herself, Ms. Frank knew now to believe Nala, especially if she was being kicked out of tutoring for whispering to a peer.

"You make it sound like she was murdering someone," Ms.

Frank exclaimed. "I am bringing this to the principal and the school board! Nala, get in the car!"

At that moment I felt scared and defensive. I couldn't believe I had been spoken to that way when I was simply trying to uphold the school's expectation of students not talking in line. After tutoring I broke down and cried. Instead of feeling sorry for myself, however, which I often did, I felt something different. I felt remorse. I felt guilty and a need to make things better. I tried to put myself in Ms. Frank's shoes and was blown away by how mad I was at myself. She was right. How dare I speak to her daughter that way. How dare I speak to other people's children that way. Nala was at tutoring to get help she desperately needed. Her mom was not only entrusting me during the school day but also an extended school day to keep Nala safe and in an environment where she could learn. I failed Nala and her mother because of the mere five seconds Nala chose to whisper to a peer.

At that moment, I realized I needed to change. That evening I mustered the courage to call Nala's mom. She didn't pick up, so I texted. I remember her response, "I don't want to talk to you."

"I understand," I replied. "I just need to apologize to you and Nala and want to do it in a more personal way."

Shortly after, Ms. Frank called! I humbled myself and just listened. I know this call was important, given how much of it I remember. Ms. Frank spoke to me about what it means to be a white teacher of Black students; what it means not to allow students to talk; what it means to her as a mother to send her children to school and know they are not safe because of the adults there. To Ms. Frank, I was being prejudiced and biased. I was imparting my white culture and expectations on her daughter. I was being oppressive and perpetuating racist practices.

She was right. Unconsciously, I was doing all of the above. Later in my life, especially once I had my own children, I realized how oppressive it is to never allow students to talk. This is even more problematic when there are racial dynamics at play.

While I did not have the parental perspective at that time, I still knew I was in the wrong. I apologized (a lot), thanked Ms. Frank (a lot), not just for the conversation but also for all she does as a mother; and I said she was right. I promised her I would do better. Without defending myself I asked her to put Nala on the phone. I apologized to Nala as well and promised to be better for her and all of my students.

This happened early in the spring and I can say that incident in tutoring was the last time I yelled at a student for whispering in line.

During the rest of our time together, I deliberately found moments to celebrate Nala. I would call home whenever she surpassed a goal. Nala would stay with me after school to celebrate her hard work. I entrusted her with errands and leadership opportunities. When she got distracted, I would remind her with proximity and silent hand gestures to get to work, and she would.

Not only did my relationship with Nala change but so did my relationship with Nala's mom. Ms. Frank and I were more than cordial, we were joyful and anchored in gratitude. At the end of the year, knowing I would be leaving the school, Ms. Frank and I hugged, both thanking each other. Her gratitude grounded in seeing change and my gratitude for her giving me the lesson on how I needed to change.

My Letter

Dear Nala,

One of my most humbling experiences as an educator occurred the year I was your teacher. Perhaps you recall there was a moment when I yelled at you during tutoring and re-moved you for talking. Little did I know your mom was right there listening and was taken aback by how I treated you.

Having you as my student, I learned it is imperative to think first in response to "unmet expectations." No person deserves to be on the receiving end of yelling. Particularly for something so small.

I learned it is further imperative to reflect on the impact my words and tone can have on people. Is it ever okay to yell? Not over the things I was yelling at you for.

I learned the importance of swallowing my pride, facing my fear, and listening. Your mom might have wanted to yell at me and report my behavior to the board. Instead, she let me apologize. She forgave me and asked me to be better. Thanks to her forgiveness, I committed to doing better.

With Gratitude,

Ms. Adams

Lessons and Resources

When you are in the wrong, own it

If we as teachers are in the wrong we have to own it. It is not our principals' responsibility to take on all of our issues. Our students' families should not feel they have to tattle on us but rather should feel they can come to us with concerns. They should know we will listen to them and, if we have done something wrong, we will hold ourselves accountable and make things right.

Be a listener first and foremost

We need to listen to our students' families. They have a voice and more often than not, they know their children better than anyone. Even if their tone starts off confrontational this is often because they are coming from a place of love. Typically, their tone will change once we demonstrate genuine care and concern for their children and an ability to take responsibility for our actions. Remember to engage in active and compassionate listening, reflecting back when appropriate, to really make sure you understand your students' and family members' concerns.

I will add that, as your safety is also important, if you ever feel unsafe in an interaction, you should certainly leave. That being said, for white teachers working in primarily Black communities, oftentimes feelings of safety can be distorted. People in this country have been conditioned to be afraid of Black people so a white teacher being confronted by an angry or hurt, Black parent may feel more "unsafe" than if that same parent were white. It is important to be mindful of this as you endeavor to really listen to your students and their families.

Work on You

The littlest things set me off as a teacher. The second a student did not "comply" with my expectations I detonated, reacting in an explosive way. In Nala's case, she was merely whispering when I expected silence. I don't even know what she was talking about.

Many of us have likely heard the saying, "don't sweat the small stuff." But in education, via the mantra of *Teach Like a Champion*, we learn it is in fact important to " sweat the small stuff," especially if a student is talking when they aren't supposed to. As teachers we're taught not to expect marginal compliance but, instead, to nip the unwanted behavior in the bud. There are ways, however, to react that are much more humanizing and supportive.

If you are a ticking time bomb like me, and you know your fuse is short, it doesn't mean you shouldn't be an educator but it does mean there is inner work you have to do to help control it. I have had to train myself to breathe, to look at the situation differently. I will force a smile or even a giggle just to diffuse the situation. I meditate every morning. Sometimes even in the afternoons when all the little things are piling up and I am about to lose it. I did a lot of work on my classroom when I was a teacher, and I made progress, but I only made so much. That is, until I actually started working on myself. If at any point you stagnate or digress as a teacher, then it is time to look within and really begin the self-work!

CHAPTER 10

My Turn Around Story

"I CAN'T DO IT! I CAN'T DO IT! ARE YOU HAPPY NOW?"

Those words still ring in my head and hurt my heart. They were the words that changed my teaching philosophy and practices. David was the student who changed my life.

I met David in 2008. He was entering fifth grade and being raised by his grandma. His mom was still in the picture but was sick and confined to a wheelchair and therefore was unable to care for David. His grandmother worked for the Charlotte-Mecklenburg public transportation system and, to my surprise, since our school did not have school busses David, an 11-year-old, would take the public bus to and from school. At the time, in my late-twenties-white-woman mind I thought, "How could a family do that to their child?" I didn't realize until years later that this question was fueled by judgment and unconscious bias. Sadly, that wasn't the only time unconscious bias and judgment crept into my interactions with David and his grandmother. I remember at one point, while in math class, I was reprimanding David for not finishing his homework and told him I would have to call his grandma and let her know he had to stay after school until he completed his work. His grandmother asked to talk to him. I handed him the phone and he said, "Don't make me stay with this woman. If you do, I am going to run from this school." You would think that would have been a wake up call for me but it only added fuel to my fire.

I should mention, when David entered fifth grade he had just tested out of receiving Special Education services. This meant he no longer had access to the legally-required accommodations and modifications like extra time, modified homework, and various other ways to support his learning. Nonetheless, his diagnostic scores indicated he still seriously needed support, as he was at least three years behind in math and reading, putting him at a second-grade level. And while our school did offer some interventions, it wasn't enough.

I can recall even more stories of tension with David and ways I looked down on him, his circumstances, and his family. In my mind, whatever was getting in the way of his success never had anything to do with me. After all, my heart was in this. Six years earlier I had been admitted into a prominent and highly selective organization that was working to dismantle educational inequity. I was the founding math teacher at a school with predominantly Black students. I was passionate, working 12-16 hour days and I wanted to save the world through education. It wasn't until sometime in the third quarter (that is over six and a half years into my teaching career) that I finally stopped and heard what David had to say about how he was feeling. It took him being vulnerable, at the risk of being embarrassed in front of his classmates, that I *finally* listened.

I was supervising David and about 20 to 25 other fifth graders in homework detention one afternoon. Imagine having what could be interpreted as the least engaged students and/or the students with the highest learning needs all in one space. It was overwhelming, like playing the most challenging game of whack-a-mole. Students asking for help, hands constantly up, some students just taking the opportunity to play knowing this would be over at some point and we couldn't keep them there all night. It was most unproductive and while I didn't and wouldn't have thought to own it at the time, the lack of productivity was because of me.

At one point David had gotten out of his seat after I had already told him multiple times to go back and sit down. I had finally had it. That was my last straw. I remember yelling (full on college-basketball-coach yelling) something to the effect of, "David, ARE YOU KIDDING ME? SIT DOWN, NOW! DO YOUR WORK, NOW! DO BETTER, NOW! I AM SICK OF SOUNDING LIKE A BROKEN RECORD WITH YOU! IF YOU DON'T SIT DOWN, YOU WILL BE HERE TOMORROW!"

"Tomorrow" happened to be Saturday. Not only was I ready to "punish" David, apparently I was ready to punish myself. Thinking he would go back to his seat, you can imagine my surprise when I was met with a rebuttal, one that mirrored my tone and also my volume. It wasn't vindictive, hurtful, or angry, but rather pleading.

David yelled back, "I CAN'T DO IT! I CAN'T DO IT! ARE YOU HAPPY NOW?" He threw the work at me. Tears were running down his face. The other students weren't quite sure what to do. The culture of our school was if a student talked back to a teacher, there were consequences.

I felt the desire to yell back but, uncharacteristically, I didn't. As I watched David sob and as I looked around the room for a moment, I realized all this time I had been punishing him for being behind, which was not even his fault. I was punishing him for needing help. He wasn't getting out of his seat to be disrespectful. He *needed* help. He *wanted* help. And I was not giving it to him.

That afternoon David's grandmother was coming to pick him up. Before she arrived, I knew I owed David an apology. I remember sitting down with him in the classroom next door and simply saying, "I am so sorry." He was seemingly and rightfully surprised by this and also likely didn't trust it. Seeing him standing there, bearing his truth in front of his classmates, I knew I was in the wrong. I was so caught up in feeling that he was disrespecting me. In reality I had disrespected him time and time again when all he needed was to be heard and helped.

I continued to apologize, trying to ensure he heard and felt my sincerity. We ended up talking for quite a while and I did everything in my power to ask and listen and share my gratitude for his vulnerability. While the conversation was fruitful, I knew it would take a lot more to earn his and his grandmother's trust. When his grandmother arrived, I also apologized to her. Expressing, for the sake of David and his education, which was so clearly important to both of them, I would be better. I had to be better.

It took time, but I kept my commitment and, within weeks, David was asking to stay after school and getting help. His grandmother and I worked out a schedule and we made sure David was getting the support he needed both during and after school. Some evenings he would stay with me until 6 pm. We would find leftover lunches and make sure he ate dinner. He would complete his homework and we would work on concepts he still needed to master. While the academic time was amazing, the most special time was when he had finished all his work and we would help put the school back together, cleaning up classrooms, sharpening pencils, and putting away chairs in the "cafegymatoriam." Not only did I learn he was (and is) a very bright student who needed different types of support, I also learned he had one of the biggest hearts.

My Letter

Dear David,

That moment in homework detention was a turning point for me as a teacher. I have taken that lesson with me and share it with as many people who need it. When coaching teachers who I see losing their patience with students, I always ask them, "Could you imagine being a student and not understanding something? I think I would act out too."

David, you need to know those last few months of working together, seeing you grow, and just learning what an amazing human being you are, I likely learned more from you than you ever did from me.

You and your grandma taught me that getting on a public bus to travel to and from school is not a sign of neglectful or irresponsible parenting; it shows commitment to your education! It shows how much you and your grandma were willing to invest in your education. And, it shows your capacity to learn and navigate beyond the four walls of a classroom. I am not even sure how many adults can take public transportation successfully. I for one was not privy or skilled at understanding the complexities and yet, there you were, an 11-year-old navigating Charlotte, NC and its public transportation system like a pro. Brilliance!

You taught me to consider first why a student might be "acting out" and to give them grace and find ways to understand where they are coming from before they have to blow up to be heard. No student should ever have to do that, and I am so sorry you had to with me.

You taught me there is so much to a person's story and we should never make assumptions about the students we are teaching. Teachers must take the time to get to know their students deeply and never blame students when they enter their classroom behind in their learning. Had I taken the time to realize this early on, I often wonder how much more learning would have taken place.

You are a source of inspiration to me and I am so proud to say I know you and I am grateful to everything you have taught me.

Humbly,
Ms. Adams

Lessons and Resources

Check your biases
When you are teaching students, especially those who don't share your background, it is not enough to simply love kids to be a transformational teacher. Early on, my desire to become a teacher was because I loved kids but I soon learned during my first year of teaching that I loved *most* kids. I was not only harboring racial biases but gender biases as well. For instance, when I got my first female student (during the later

part of my first year of teaching) the boys in my class made it all too clear they could tell I preferred Angela over them. While I initially denied it, I eventually realized I did in fact treat my female students with much more regard and the first time I had a group of white female students I treated them even better. I was kinder, I would never think to raise my voice with them and when we had an issue we talked about it.

That is what bias looks like. We all have bias and it plays out differently for each of us. This is especially true, and harmful, in school settings. Until I was explicitly told and trained on how to consider my privileges, how to look my biases head on, I denied those biases existed. One thing that changed this for me was reading "Why are All the Black Kids Sitting Together in the Cafeteria?" by Beverly Tatum. If you haven't read it, I highly encourage you to do so, and quickly.

Know and understand your students

When teaching students, it is imperative we get to know, truly know them. I made assumptions about David and his family that only made our relationship more contentious. If we are to truly educate our students, they need to know we value them and see their assets. Be sure to get to know your students and their families deeply.

Notice, I will NEVER use the term "parent" exclusively, unless I know that to be true of a family dynamic because David's family helped reinforce the reality that those who raised us are not necessarily those who birthed us. I challenge you to change your words from exclusively "Parent" to "Family(ies)." For example, instead of "Parent Teacher Conference" be more inclusive and say "Family Teacher Conference."

Be asset-based

Our students might come to us with deficits, every person has them, we are human. Our students, however, also come to us with even greater strengths and we have to know what those strengths are beyond just how students learn. In David's story, for instance, I neglected to see his strengths in building friendships as well as navigating the city of Charlotte through the public transportation system. He brought so much with him to the school and when tapped into, he was able to learn so much more!

Moving Forward

CHAPTER 11

Transformation Comes When You Are Most Uncomfortable

"Can't having a good heart, having good intentions, and wanting to make things better be enough?"

This was a question I asked out loud at my initial training to become a coach of teachers. I never expected the level of pushback I received. I realize now, however, how naïve my comment was.

In 2009 I left the classroom. That was one of the hardest decisions of my life. I found myself burned out. In fact, I found myself passed out in the United States Capitol and then spending the remainder of our fifth-grade field trip to Washington D.C. in the hospital and in the care of a friend.

While I knew it was time to leave the classroom, my heart would not let me leave education so I applied to be a teacher coach with a non-profit. When they offered me the position, I readily accepted it and began my training. To my surprise, my initial training did not cover the technicalities of how to coach but, rather, who I am as a coach. Specifically, a white female primarily coaching white teachers who would be teaching students of color.

Like many people, I didn't quite understand why this type of identity work was so important and, as you read at the start of this chapter, my wondering was outward. Thankfully, I had a manager who was ready and willing to have tough conversations with me. She wanted to support me in my development and was not willing to give up on me as she knew this exploration was imperative to my coaching career and intended impact.

One of the first things she had me do was read Beverly Tatem's "Why are All the Black Kids Sitting Together in the Cafeteria?" I devoured the book and while our check-ins did cover some of the technicalities of coaching, we spent the majority of the time discussing identity and what it means to be a white female educator working in marginalized communities of color.

While the work I had been doing for the previous seven years was in these very communities and, as you know from the journey I shared with you in the first two parts of the book, I spent some time taking good hard looks at myself, my deepest reflections came during this training time with my manager.

In reading Tatum's work and engaging in meaningful dialogue with one of the most extraordinary educational leaders I have ever worked with, I had some of the most profound realizations and lessons.

It was in this reading that I learned about the concept of white identity development (table below). I remember reading this over and over and over again and assessing where I was on this continuum. In this realization, I also pondered my comment at the beginning of my training and what that comment meant. I was in "Stage 1" and had a long way to go in my role as a white educator working with students of color despite the previous seven years.

White Racial Identity Model

Stage 1: CONTACT	In the first stage of contact, the individual adheres to the "colorblind" motto. They see racial difference but do not find it salient and, in fact, may feel that racism is propagated by the discussion and acknowledgement of race as an issue. In this stage, there is no conscious demonstration of racism here. This seemingly non-racist position can cover unconscious racist beliefs. If the individual is confronted with real-world experiences or knowledge that uncovers the privileges of White skin, they may move into the disintegration stage.

Stage 2: DISINTEGRATION

In this stage, because the person has new experiences which confront his prior conception of the world and because this conception is now challenged by this new information or experience, the person is often plagued by feelings of guilt and shame. These emotions of guilt and shame can be modified when the person decides to channel these emotions in a positive way but when those emotions continue to dominate, the person may move into the re-integration stage.

Stage 3: REINTEGRATION

This stage is marked by a "blame-the-victim" attitude that's more intense than anything experienced in the contact stage. They may feel that, although white people do have privilege, it is probably because they deserve them and are in some way superior to minority groups. If the person is able to combat these feelings, they may be able to move on to the pseudo-independence stage

**Stage 4:
PSEUDO-
INDEPENDENCE**

**Stage 5:
IMMERSION/
EMERSION**

This is the first stage of positive racial identification. Although an individual in this stage does not feel that white people deserve privilege, they look to people of color, not themselves, to confront and uncover racism. They approve of these efforts and comfort the person as these efforts validate this person's desire to be non-racist. Although this is positive white racial identity, the person does not have a sense of how they can be both white and non-racist together.

In this stage, the person makes a genuine attempt to connect to his/her own white identity and to be anti-racist. This stage is usually accompanied by deep concern with understanding and connecting to other white people who are or have been dealing with issues of racism.

<table>
<tr><td>Stage 6: AUTONOMY</td><td>The last stage is reached when an individual has a clear understanding of and positive connection to their white racial identity while also actively pursuing social justice. Helms' stages are as much about finding a positive racial identification with being white and becoming an active anti-racist.</td></tr>
</table>

(Helms, 1992)

In conversations with my manager, I never felt like she was watering down my understanding of this topic in order to placate my feelings. When I realized where I was in my own identity development, she agreed and let me know she would support me in becoming better.

As my team grew more diverse, I was held even more accountable. Instead of being silent and carrying guilt, I asked questions and tried to take responsibility for my ignorance. I tried humbly to understand and the more I worked to understand, the harder I tried to help support the teachers I coached in their own understanding.

Of course, being human, I continued to make mistakes

but I finally had a team calling me in and supporting my development. I remember sitting down with another team member who, like my manager, saw my efforts and potential but also saw the mistakes I was making. She and I met at a local bakery and her words still resound in my heart:

Colleague: *I really appreciate you asking me to coffee. I know that had to be hard for you after you saw me visibly upset at our meeting.*

Me: *Thanks for taking the time to meet with me. I respect you so much and want to be better.*

Colleague: *I know you do, and I hear you apologize for your mistakes and I see you doing better. I am just so tired. I feel like the staff members of color are over utilized. We are constantly having to be the ones who lead the Diversity, Equity, and Inclusion (DEI) work. We have staff members like yourself who are coming to these realizations but still require so much support. I just want people to get it and take more off our shoulders. There is too much at stake and when we [people of color] have to give so much to our colleagues, how are we to sustain in the work we are doing?*

What she was describing in essence was "Stage 4." I was overly reliant and was not actually using my own privilege to support the work toward educational equity. It was time I leaned in more. After all, I was being called in. I needed to accept the invitation. I realized when I was confronted with comments similar to the ones I was making in my initial days of training, I did not need to instantly look to my colleagues of color to address the issue. It was up to me to have these conversations.

I work daily to be an anti-racist, an ally, an accomplice. I likely would not be where I am today, even writing this book, had I not left the classroom, had I not had the manager I was assigned, had I not read Tatum. Perhaps I still would have gotten to where I am but my guess is, my journey would have been much longer. Who's to say? What I do know is, every day, I aspire to be better. I wake up cognizant of my privileges and work alongside so many people who are also looking at themselves in the mirror and deciding that who they are has everything to do with the change we want and need to see in education.

My Letter

To My Former Manager and Colleagues,

Wow, thank you! Thank you for making me uncomfortable. Thank you for holding me accountable. Thank you for caring for me through all my faults, forgiving me and pushing me to be better. I know I am far from perfect and every day I have to show up to be accepted as an ally and accomplice. I know I have to continue looking at myself, considering who I am and what I need to do to be better.

I realize, it is not people of color's responsibility to bear the burden of talking about race, injustice, and identity. I have immense responsibility as a leader in education to do more and commit to taking the burden off my peers.

Because of you all, I have learned as educators, especially white educators, well-intentioned kindness is not enough. I must continually explore my identity as a white woman in America, critically examining the ways I perpetuate (consciously or unconsciously) white supremacy and racism.

While I understood the beauty and difficulty in teaching in an environment far different than the environments in which I was educated and further understood these environments were under-resourced as a function of racism, I didn't realize how I was perpetuating the problem by not looking at myself beyond my good intentions.

Because of you all, I learned I had (have) a lot more work to do to address how I contribute to structural racism. I learned I wanted to be part of the solution and that meant starting with me.

In debt and immense gratitude,

Kelley

Lessons Learned

"Loving" children is not enough

In the article "Dear White Teachers: You Can't Love Your Black Students If You Don't Know Them" Bettina Love explains, "The question is not: Do you love all children? The question is: Will you fight for justice for Black and Brown children? And how will you fight?"

I once thought my love and passion for children was enough. I learned (far too long after I had begun teaching), however, that when we as white women teach in communities different from the ones we were raised in, we have to do more than just love our students. We have to be willing to join the "fight" and while fighting isn't likely something people like myself were raised to do, I also recognize that if I am not showing up in ways that support and uplift the liberation of the most marginalized groups in our country, I am likely perpetuating the problem.

When reading Tatum's book I had the further realization (for the first time in almost ten years of education) that being a teacher is NOT missionary work. This is not us coming to impart our values and beliefs on students of color but, instead, working alongside our students, their families, and their communities. And, more often than not, it will require us as educators to be willing to take the passenger seat and allow our students, their families, and communities to lead.

Love shares, "I argue that you must fight with the

creativity, imagination, urgency, boldness, ingenuity, and rebellious spirit of abolitionists to advocate for an education system where all Black and Brown children are thriving. I call this abolitionist teaching. To love all children, we must struggle together to create the schools we are taught to believe are impossible: Schools built on justice, love, joy, and anti-racism."

Are you ready to fight? Are you ready to struggle? Are you ready to create schools we have been taught are impossible? I know I am!

I highly recommend reading Bettina Love's essays and books as not only does she tell it like it is, she does so in inspiring and actionable ways.

We have to be okay with being uncomfortable

Author of "Racial Healing Handbook" (2019), Anneliese A. Singh suggests becoming a white anti-racist person means "taking responsibility for your power and privilege, acknowledging the feelings you have to increase multiculturalism, cultivating a desire for understanding and growth, etc. "

I will admit, at first when I received feedback on my comments around race and how they made people feel, I was very uncomfortable. I agree that when it comes to race, racism, and anti-racist work, it is important everyone feels safe, but equally important that many also feel uncomfortable. "It's only through discomfort, perhaps pain and suffering, that we grow, develop, and change for the better." (Condon & Young, 2017)

For those of us who know how it feels to make a mistake or fail, we know how uncomfortable that can feel. We also likely know, however, that when we choose to view that mistake or failure as a learning opportunity, we grow.

Keep moving forward. Don't shy away from these critical conversations. They are too important not to have if we are going to work to build a truly equal educational system.

If you have not already, please read Beverly Tatum's book "Why are all the Black Kids Sitting in the Cafeteria?" This was my life-changing book, and perhaps it can be yours as well.

CHAPTER 12

Wake Up!

"The teacher is of course an artist, but being an artist does not mean that he or she can make the profile, can shape the students. What the educator does in teaching is to make it possible for the students to become themselves."
—— **Paulo Friere (2000)**

In the spring of 2010, two women, one a realtor and entrepreneur, the other me, an educator, sat in a local coffee shop getting to know one another, talking about real estate and other things. Then the conversation took a turn.

Realtor / Entrepreneur: "What does it mean to bring students to the forefront of this movement?"

Me: "It means we allow our students to understand what education inequity is and provide them space to decide what they want to do about it."

This conversation happened a few months after I started coaching teachers full time. You see, I had fallen in love with my job, but just as I was taking into account and putting into action all I had learned over the course of my time in the classroom, there was something missing and that was students.

Prior to the above question my realtor friend posed, she first asked me, "If you could do anything, what would you do?"

"I am doing it," I replied. "I absolutely love coaching teachers."

She pressed on and said, "Okay, but is there anything else you would want to do that you aren't doing?"

I thought about it for a few seconds, considered what was missing in my life and responded, "I would bring students to the forefront of this movement, having them work alongside their teachers and adults in their lives."

Those questions she asked, that less than five-minute conversation, put into motion a platform that not only changed my life trajectory but the lives of the teachers I was working alongside, as well as their students. The result was a program called Wake Up! Students for Educational Equity (Wake Up!).

I began talking to local leaders who were working in education with an emphasis on equity, from school administrators to non-profit leaders, entrepreneurs, and even local and state government officials. I connected with students at local colleges who cared deeply about social justice, particularly in regards to education, and suddenly I was founding a program for students. I created a steering committee composed of adults, college interns, and high school students. We were now working in partnership with a non-profit called "The Possibility Project." We were coming together weekly and building what we eventually called a *Student Empowerment Summit.*

Early into the project, one of the college interns on the steering committee and I spent the day together, driving around the city, stopping at schools, and interviewing middle and high school students about what it meant to have an excellent education. That evening, the intern and his roommate compiled and edited content and created audio. Suddenly we had a promotional video to share with the masses and get more students involved.

As we promoted the summit, we started reaching out to local philanthropists and raised money to support the event. In a span of two weeks we had raised $20,000 as the community was willing to invest in its future!

Now, I don't mean to make any of this sound easy. I was working 65+ hours a week, but I have found that passion = productivity.

Ten months from the date of that initial conversation in a coffee shop, we had our first cohort of students sitting in an auditorium-style classroom at Queen's College in Charlotte, North Carolina. The two-day summit consisted of approximately 70 students from across the Charlotte-Mecklenburg School system and over 20 educators listening to speakers, a panel of local educational and political leaders and our keynote speaker, Dr. Earnest Morrell. We also offered a college access support seminar. At the end of the second day, the student groups had the opportunity to meet, reflect, and strategize about what they had learned.

The weekend was powerful. At the summation of the event, our program evaluations clearly indicated we were on to something and needed to build on that momentum.

I had just had my first baby, he was a mere 6 weeks old at the time, so the idea of making this event bigger felt exciting but daunting. As I finished my maternity leave, however, I kept receiving outreach from people across the city saying Wake Up! needed to keep happening as it was what our young community needed.

The steering committee took a month off before returning to our regularly scheduled meetings. I wrote a proposal to the Executive Director of the organization I was working for at the time and asked for $30,000 in funding for Wake Up!, offering it as part of our programming for the teachers our organization supported. My Executive Director said "yes" and year two was underway.

This time, the summit wasn't a single weekend, it was two in-person gatherings at different local colleges and a club-like opportunity for our students in classrooms across CMS schools. This time we had approximately 100 students participating.

The summit took place at our convention center where we once again hosted a panel with state and local school board representatives, educational non-profit leaders, and the school system's superintendent.

Whereas the first summit had adults speaking to students, this time we had the students speaking to adults. *The Possibility Project* did a poetic presentation on what educational inequity and the pursuit of equity meant to them. Students from each school presented to adults, in breakout sessions, what they learned from conducting a SWOT (Strengths, Weaknesses, Opportunities, Threats) analysis at their schools and began to determine how they as an educational equity group could build and support programming at their schools.

That is where that year's program ended -- at the summit. Poetically, this makes sense, given that when people reach the summit of a hike, they have arrived at their ultimate destination. There was no follow-up action, however, just talking. A summit couldn't be our destination point without something more meaningful before it.

Seeing what students were able to think about as

opportunities and pain points for their communities and schools, we wondered what else they could do with more time. We wanted this work to be so much more than a summit. We wanted our time together to have an impact. So, again, we took our two-week break and decided to adjust course and make the summit an actual program. This time, schools would put the conversations into motion by completing Action Projects. And these projects would happen before the summit.

In our third year we were building students' capacity, not just to recognize strengths and areas of need but to take action and actually work with their community toward progress. The programming, created and supported by our steering committee, was now weekly and easily digestible by teachers and students. The clubs came together after school once a week and, beginning in September, the entire Wake Up! community came together once a month to help build knowledge, skills, and mindsets around self-awareness and community understanding. We spent our first gathering building community and getting to know each other.

We did a "privilege walk," an activity where participants confront the ways in which society privileges some individuals over others. This is designed to help participants reflect on the different areas in their lives where they have privilege as well as the areas they don't. We also had students engage in a "cross the line" activity, identifying and eliminating the barriers between people that perpetuate acts of unkindness. We were building a culture of understanding and honoring our differences and ourselves. Students who were white were standing in front of Black and brown students, asking themselves what it means to be a white person in our society, wondering for the first time, what privilege really does mean in our country. Students of color for the first time were engaging in dialogue with students outside their schools about what it meant to be a person of color in America. All of this was now student led.

In the third year, our reach extended further and we partnered with the teen group "The Intersection," where founder and executive director Zeke Cohen brought his own teens down from Baltimore, MD to share their content and programming. That first day, we started with self. Students and teachers wrote their story of self. They wrote about who they were, why, and what that meant in terms of how they showed up and were represented in education. One of our students shared her status as a DACA student (Deferred Action for Childhood Arrivals), which meant she was undocumented and wondered if she would be able to attend college as a result of her immigration status. Students and teachers wrote, they read, they revised and they shared vulnerably, poetically, and powerfully.

In November 2013, we gathered at Johnson C. Smith University, a historically black college, and shared virtual school visits. The task from October to November was for school groups to spend that month recording students, staff, hallways, pep-rallies; really anything that would give people outside of their school community a broadened understanding of the strengths, weaknesses, opportunities, and threats of their own school. Some students were perplexed that one school had catered lunches a few times a week from local restaurants, while others were surprised that the majority of students at some schools received free lunch. Students saw for the first time what it looked like for a school to be majority students of color and have rich culture and pride. They were confronted with their biases and had to reflect on what those biases meant for them.

And in December, we engaged an artist's depiction of inequitable education and oppression over time in America. Students gathered on the campus of UNC-Charlotte and silently walked around two rooms reflecting on pictures that said more than words. These were the pictures of the people who came before them, who endured a fight for freedom, for justice, for equality. Students were given journals and the prompts:

- *What are these pictures making you think or feel?*
- *Are there any pictures that bring up added emotion? If so, which one(s)? Describe the emotion.*

People don't believe me when I say a group of 100 students can be silent for over 45 minutes without the presence of technology but that day the silence was real, it was impenetrable. Students saw how our country treated people of color... they questioned why. We engaged in deep, meaningful conversations around that very question. That afternoon, we watched *Mighty Times: The Children's March* (2004). While the day was powerful, we were only scratching the surface.

Tom Torlino, a Carlisle School student, before and after spending time at the school.
(Choate, 1885)

(Immigration Impact, n.d.)

Mother (Nettie Hunt) and daughter (Nickie) sit on steps of the Supreme Court building on May 18, 1954, the day following the Court's historic decision in Brown v. Board of Education. Nettie is holding a newspaper with the headline "High Court Bans Segregation in Public Schools."
(Bettman, 1954)

One of the Little Rock Nine, Elizabeth Eckford on her first
day of school.
(Bettmann/ Getty Images, 1957)

U.S. Army troops escort nine black students out of Little
Rock's Central High School.
(Bettmann/ Getty Images, 1957)

US deputy marshals escort 6-year-old Ruby Bridges from William Frantz
Elementary School in New Orleans.
(Uncredited DOJ Photographer- Public Domain, 1960)

Lunch Counter Sit-In
(Blackwell, 1963)

The Children's Crusade
(Charles Moore/ Getty Images, 1963)

In four months we had worked to build self-love, community, and awareness, all in an effort to build our students' capacity to lead in the fight for educational equity and, that year, our students did not disappoint. From January to April students worked tirelessly and put into action profoundly inspiring projects that truly changed the trajectory of education.

One middle school began to recognize a lack of diversity in their honors classes. While the majority of the school was students of color, primarily Black, the honors classes had majority white students. At this realization, these young scholars began asking questions. Why was this the case? Has this always been the case? Did other people, including families, know what an honors track could mean for students' futures? In this pursuit for answers, they decided to educate. At their monthly family nights, they set up a table at the front entrance and asked these very questions. Their goal: increase the number / percentage of students of color in honors classes.

Another high school wondered about the pattern of suspensions and expulsions, realizing students who were getting suspended were disproportionately males of color, and primarily Black males, even though the school had majority students who identified as Hispanic and/or Latinx. This especially came to light when a white female student got in trouble for something a male student of color had previously been suspended for. The female was suspended for less time than the male student and neither had a prior disciplinary history. That group of students began asking for data, digging deeply into the district's historical trends and discipline policies. As part of their action, they presented at a school board meeting to ensure those writing and ultimately overseeing the district's policies were aware of the disparate numbers and asked that the school board review their discipline policy and revise it to make it more equitable. They did!

A different participating high school looked closely at the school's attrition and the lessening numbers of students over time. How could their freshman classes in some years have 50% more students than that of their senior classes? What was happening to the upperclassmen? As they worked to answer these questions, they learned that while people often bring up the idea of students "dropping out," they adopted the idea of students being "pushed out." Over time, students found themselves less successful in school and, once again, the push out rate was disproportionately high for males of color. With this realization, the high school group built a mentorship program with one of their feeder middle schools in hopes of supporting them in academics and culture. They went down to the middle school monthly and, as students entered high school, these mentorships continued.

One last action project that garnered great momentum was that of a well-performing charter school where many students were provided post-graduate opportunities to attend prestigious colleges on scholarships. The school, while in

Mecklenburg County, was outside of Charlotte. The majority of students were white and from middle- or upper-class families. Students at this school realized what a privilege it was to attend and began to question their own privilege. Why were they afforded certain opportunities many other students, particularly those of color who deserve the same level of education, were not? They realized it had to do with location and access. Therefore, this group of young teens decided (1) they wanted more students of color to know about the school and (2) they wanted to partner with people in the communities of students of color to provide them access. The teens spent Saturdays and Sundays in Charlotte, talking to local pastors about the school. The pastors in return brought in students who were looking for a college prep education.

These are merely four of the projects from that year. Seeing these actions and the ways they transformed educational spaces in our community was a great way to say goodbye to this passion project.

That was my final year with Wake Up! It was the spring of 2014. At the final summit we had nearly 350 guests, which included our Governor's Educational Director, students, teachers, and local and statewide leaders. Our students and teachers stood and shared their stories, the ones they began to write in October. Schools presented their action projects. The Possibility Project performed and, finally, audience members shared the mic, naming their commitments to educational equity with the group. One commitment made by the governor's educational director was to have true representation of students at a state level as long as he held that role. That individual upheld his promise.

I share the timeline and stories from Wake Up! in this book because this was my passion project. Wake Up! was a culmination of all the things I had done wrong and all the lessons I had learned as a teacher and actually made better. I was putting into practice those hard lessons and realities I have shared with you throughout this book. All because one person asked me, "If you could do anything, what would you do?"

So I ask you, what would you do if you could do anything?

My Letter

Dear Wake-Up Founders and Participants,

Making the move to Colorado was one of the hardest decisions I have ever made as I knew it meant leaving one of the most rewarding experiences of my life: Wake Up!

In our time together I was pushed to see students as young people who had so much to offer this world. I was introduced to true representation and how we as a society too often tokenize our students versus leaning on them to be thought leaders and our peers.

I learned it takes a village of diverse voices to make a movement and I learned that with these diverse voices movement can and will happen. In these differences, I also learned some hard lessons in humility and how to recognize when it is time for me to sit down, be quiet, and listen.

I learned there is power in numbers and when you have a group of brilliant and diverse perspectives and ages, mindsets shift and true learning happens. We were intentional in not just having marginalized schools represented but also some of our most affluent schools at the table. We had DACA students alongside legacy students guaranteed to go to some of the most prestigious colleges in the state of NC sitting side by side, sharing their stories and engaging in dialogue. And in this diversity and numbers we had groups supporting one another in profound ways.

I was introduced to *Critical Pedagogy* and saw not only light bulbs going on for students but also for their teachers who realized the capacity our students hold.

Wake Up! changed my life. I know my time in the classroom and all the stories I shared earlier in this book helped inform this transformation. Had I not had the struggles and hard lessons, this likely would have never happened. I would have stopped at students sitting and listening to adults. But we didn't. We kept on and because of the extraordinary leadership of teachers willing to become facilitators and students willing and ready to step up, we did so much to improve the futures of students in Charlotte.

Thank you to each and every one of you who poured so much time and effort into making this program come to life. I am better because of you and stand in awe of the commitment you all gave to this spark of an idea. Today, given what you all are doing... that spark burns as a flame, ignited in hope, love, and belief in educational equity.

Mad Love, Respect, and, of course, Humility,

Kelley

Lessons and Resources

Critical Pedagogy is a powerful way to approach education

The concept of *Critical Pedagogy* was championed by historical educational figure Paulo Freire who shared the belief that teaching should challenge learners to examine power structures and patterns of inequality within the status quo.

Freire, in his book "Pedagogy of the Oppressed," (2000) shared:

It is not surprising that the banking concept of education regards men as adaptable, manageable beings. The more students work at storing the deposits entrusted to them, the less they develop the critical consciousness which would result from their intervention in the world as transformers of that world. The more completely they accept the passive role imposed on them, the more they tend simply to adapt to the world as it is and to the fragmented view of reality deposited in them.

Before Wake Up! and meeting Nikkea Wiler, I thought of teaching as a banking system. I am not proud to admit it but I thought teachers were supposed to stand in front of the room and deposit knowledge into their students' minds and lives. As we were building out Wake Up!, however, I learned students hold so much more insight than I ever imagined. They learned far more from each other than they did from the adults in the room. When provided the access and opportunities to make change, those changes were impactful one thousand times over. The students who participated in Wake Up! have truly gone on to be exceptional young adults. I believe so much of this is because we treated them like the exceptional people they were in the first place.

Imagine a world where, in education, all students are treated with respect and all their gifts seen as strengths. How different would the experiences, especially of our most marginalized communities, be?

Students are not to be tokenized

I learned so much through Wake Up!, especially from one of the most brilliant, beautiful people I have ever met, Ms. Nikkea Wiler. I would be remiss if I did not call her out in this book. She truly changed the way I see the world, especially the way I see young people. She was the Managing and Artistic

Director of The Possibility Project and co-founder of Wake Up! She made sure students were not only on but led the steering committee. Alongside Nikkea, students learned to facilitate and lead our Saturday sessions. She ensured we never called our student representatives "kids" but rather young people. She introduced me to the ladder of student involvement, which helped me realize how we were (or weren't) in fact leveraging our students' leadership. As mentioned above, the depth of our conversations was the result of the brilliance happening at the student level.

Please... if you are building an organization and/or program and you want students to partake, ensure those young people have a say in their role and that their role is meaningful. Students will climb up a ladder so long as they are provided the rungs. And that ladder does NOT stop at rung three (see diagram below).

Our students are so much more than tokens. They are our future and when given the opportunities to see and mold that future, great things happen. As we get older, despite the wisdom we have garnered, too often we become jaded and even molded by the status quo.

Youth does not equal lack of leadership, and we adults must always remember this.

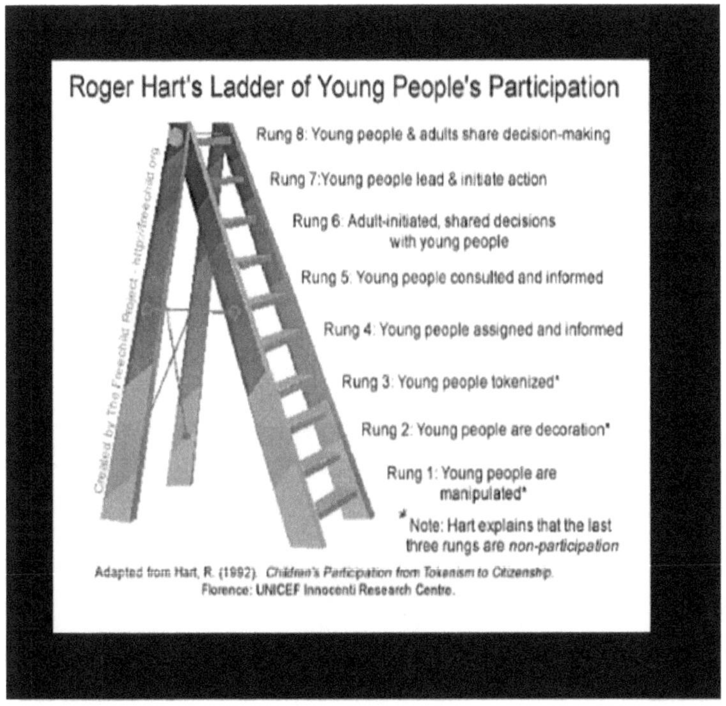

(Hart, 1992)

If you have a dream, you can build it

As I've mentioned, a beautiful human (who happened to be my realtor) asked me, "If you could do anything, what would you do?" This question was a resonating theme for our students and participants in Wake Up! We came back to this time and time again, knowing this simple question was what brought these groups of extraordinary people together.

If you could do anything to change education what would it be? Who would you need by your side to make it happen?

I found a group of highly committed, passionate adults and young people who shared the dream of an equitable education. Next to them, the movement toward educational equity felt possible.

CHAPTER 13

"This Is Not a Moment...It's a Movement" (Lin-Manuel Miranda, Hamilton)

Me: "So we are really doing this... we are moving to Colorado?"

Aaron: "I guess we are..."

In 2014 I had the privilege of participating in a fellowship that supported my leadership trajectory in the organization I was working for. In that fellowship we were cultivating our skills to become the future leaders of the organization.

At that point, I was in year three of Wake Up!, I had just had my second child, and my husband had been offered a fellowship to start an elementary school in Charlotte. His fellowship, however, would take him out of North Carolina to another state for one year. So, to keep our family together for that year of the fellowship, we decided the boys and I would follow Aaron. I began looking for different opportunities in those various cities as well as roles I could do from the luxury of my home. In my job search I stumbled upon a position that was not in any of those cities but in my hometown, Colorado Springs. This happened to be the very opportunity my own fellowship had been preparing me for, and it was with the very organization I had been working for since 2009. The job was for the Deputy Executive Director (DED) of Colorado Springs, the same city where my dad, grandparents, sister, nieces, nephew, aunts, and uncles lived. I had to go for it, although I did not expect to get the position. And then I did.

Aaron and I took a good hard look at our family and circumstances. Would we head to a city for a year as part of his fellowship and then back to Charlotte where he could fulfill his dream of starting a school or would we move to my hometown? It took us just over a month to settle on moving to Colorado.

He declined the fellowship, I accepted the job of Deputy Executive Director, and we uprooted our family (our boys were one and two at the time) and moved "home."

Upon our arrival, we decided to find a house to rent in the

school district I would be working with and Aaron landed a teaching job at a charter school in the same district. It is important to mention the school district and community in which we were living and working was (and still is) considered a "high-needs" school district in that over 80% of students receive free or reduced lunch and the majority of the students are students of color.

I stayed in the role for four years and in my final year as DED, two teachers I was supporting came to me and said they wanted to build a program for their students called "Juntos for Education." Juntos means "together" in Spanish, in other words, "together for education." The concept was to bring local students to the forefront of the conversation and movement toward educational equity. They had the vision and needed the support and resources to build it out.

I shared with them my Wake Up! Manifesto, which I had created before leaving Charlotte. It was a 14-page document outlining reflections on what I learned while founding and creating Wake Up! (much of what I am sharing with you in this book). Within months, the two teachers had Juntos up and running. We had over 50 middle- and high-school students from across southeast Colorado Springs talking about some of the most important topics around education and equity.

Like Wake Up!, teachers brought their students to Saturday workshops and we had two public events giving the student groups space to share their voices. One event took place at a local art gallery where students shared poems and letters through spoken word. They shared poetically and vulnerably how they see themselves in education and what they need as the people experiencing education this day in age. That evening we raised $2,000, all due to the students' extraordinary words.

The culminating event was held at a local college where students presented their own action projects to their families, peers, and district leadership. The amount of work students poured into this opportunity to change the course of education was beyond inspiring.

Once again, I was reminded of the power of students and also the power of teachers.

In addition to this inspiration and source of hope I also felt something deeper. I was in a state of emblazoned fury by the decisions people were making "on behalf of," but not led by, the students standing in front of me. I was fueled with righteous indignation.

I found myself at school board meetings trying to figure out why so many teachers and principals were leaving the district, the very district in which I lived, my husband worked, and my children went to school. I wanted to know what the school board was doing about it. At first these exits were disheartening, but as the numbers grew and more amazing teachers and leaders left, the more I wanted to fix this.

My tipping point was when I received a text message from one of my favorite school leaders sharing she would be leaving the district. After receiving the news, I got on the district website in hopes of connecting to the school board. I didn't have to go far. The front page of the website announced a vacancy on the board. I reached out to the president, interviewed with the directors and, in June 2018, I was appointed as a Board Director.

I learned that everyone has an agenda when they choose to run for an elected position. Even mine was to figure out how we can better train and retain excellent teachers and leaders. I don't think I could have ever anticipated what was to come. During the time of my appointment, the superintendent left the district and the board was also in conversation about a ballot measure that would provide a $180 million bond for much-needed funding for new buildings, building repairs, and technology. It had been 20 years since the last time the district had passed a bond measure. I, along with my new peers, had our work cut out for us. We needed a new superintendent, we needed to pass the bond, and we needed to help ensure the district felt a sense of commitment and pride in order to stay.

It is likely helpful to also briefly describe the role of a school board, keeping in mind that, while I was appointed, the position itself is elected. At the most basic level, school boards:

"...hire the superintendent, develop and oversee budgets,

set the school calendar, and analyze progress on a wide array of measures, all of which play a big role in how effectively and efficiently local schools serve students. They work closely with district leadership to make sure schools are running smoothly and that teachers and students get the resources they need. They deal with controversy, seek solutions to problems, and help the community come together around what matters most: making sure local kids get a world-class education." (Li Sam, 2020)

Stepping onto that board was like drinking out of a fire hose and it seemed I was learning something new daily. While my passion for teacher and leadership development and retention didn't change, I found my passions evolving. As a white woman, who had vastly different experiences than the students and community I was representing, I wanted to ensure we as a district created a platform for our students' voices and adjusted our policies to better reflect our students' needs.

It was argued that we had student "voice" and "representation" on our board because we actually had two student representatives who sat as non-voting members of the board. They applied and interviewed and were selected by the board members. When I came onto the board, I spent time with the students and asked them what they thought the board did. Their responses were in essence, "They make decisions for the district." My question back to them was, as representatives on the board, did they feel like they helped in making those decisions. Their answer was a strong, curt, "No."

When I showed them the student ladder of participation and asked what rung they would say they are on, they reflected, pondered, and answered, "Rung 3. Tokenized." They felt they were on the board so the board could say they had student representatives. At board meetings our student representatives both had time to share and, in the early part of my board experience, these students highlighted football games, homecoming, and prom. My response, "Any student can do that. Your job means so much more so let's make it more."

I believe in representation NOT tokenization. So, alongside our students, we began to build out what it meant to be a board representative. The first thing I did was actually give them our board policy book. In our first check-in we dissected the policies. During the next check-in we dug into the policies they felt they could have the most voice for. They built listening sessions at their schools, check-ins with their school administration, and, when those policies were up for discussion at our meetings, our students spoke on behalf of their constituency, specific to the board policy. They were informing us as board members how to not only adjust our policies but also how to vote on them. Our policies began to evolve! Once again, our students taught me more than I could teach them.

Beyond student voice and representation, I felt we also needed to tackle the actual representation of the senior leadership of the district and our board itself. Of the five of us, only one individual on the board was a person of color when, in fact, over 70% of the district are people of color. This was made even more evident when I sat in conversation with two white males, both district leaders:

Male 1: I don't see color. I was poor growing up and I understand what the students in the district need. I will maintain a high bar of excellence and expect our students to work hard and know they can achieve the same results I did as long as they work hard.

Male 2: Yeah, I grew up in this very community. I graduated from one of the high schools. My life was the same as our students. I was poor and had to face a lot of what our students face.

Me: Do you not think you are granted privileges as white males?

Male 2: No. I have had to work hard and believe as long as people work hard they can achieve anything. Just because I am light complected doesn't mean I didn't have to work as hard as our students who are darker than me.

Me (in thought): (He can't even call himself white?)

Male 1: I grew up poor too and with a single mom, so I know exactly what our students are going through. My skin color has nothing to do with my success.

Me: This worries me as the people who are making

decisions on part of our students. I am the mom of two white males. I can say with confidence that my children likely will not have to face the same biases that their friends will face who don't look like them. While I am a mom and will worry tirelessly about my boys, my worry will likely never be the same worry that mothers of children of color will have for their own children. I get that neither of you were fed off of a silver spoon, but that does not mean that society looks and treats you differently than they do people of color.

This conversation was beyond frustrating and the realization was startling. I began to talk about my privilege in board meetings. Some people got it, others didn't. At a meeting that occurred one week after the death of a former student who was shot and killed at the hands of the police, I shared how unsettled I was with our district policies and that what we are granting our students does little to represent who they are and their self-identified needs. We promise them an education, but does that promise them life? A diploma is not a bulletproof vest.

And further, an "education" does not guarantee our students will not face racism, bigotry, and classism. No one, not even the most liberatory education, can guarantee a healthy, successful life, especially given the society we live in.

While no education can promise life, a "quality" education (or education built from a liberation framework) can teach young people how to begin to build lives for themselves and their community that encourage wellness and can potentially decrease the likelihood they will end up in life-threatening situations (or at least can begin to challenge the factors that contribute to life-threatening situations).

We had to do better and we had an opportunity to do so. How was our district truly guaranteeing life beyond graduation?

We did manage to adjust some policies to consider the backgrounds of our students to elevate cultural differences. While I chose not to run again for this position, my hope was to leave a lasting impact on how the board considers the unique, beautiful, and brilliant voices and identities of our students and their backgrounds.

In the years my family and I moved back to Colorado, many experiences led us to realizations of what education could and should be. Likely one of the most profound experiences, however, was the loss of one of our closest friends, a fellow educator, whose greatest core value was "belief." He was someone who actually brought Aaron and me together. We worked with him, we lived with him, we founded a school with him.

Devastatingly, our friend lost his battle with cancer. His passing shook us to our core. His funeral in New Jersey displayed the last healthy picture of him, which was at the Richard Rodgers Theater where "Hamilton" had opened. Following the funeral, Aaron insisted we were going to the theater to watch "Hamilton," as it reminded him of the work we did alongside one another. I did not want to go. I was sad, and sick, and thousands of miles away from my boys. But we went and that night changed my life. In fact, that entire weekend was powerful in loss and beginnings. That weekend I committed myself to carrying on the passion our friend had ignited in so many people. As I sat on the board, as I made decisions on behalf of students, I continuously channeled his strength, courage, and belief. With that, I leave this letter in the spirit of both my dear friend, who has helped shape how I lead in the space of education and the profound words of "Hamilton." (Miranda, 2015)

My Letter

Dear Teachers, Administrators, Community Members, and Former Colleagues,

"This is not a moment, it's a movement"- I joined this work as a teacher in 2002- connected to the mission, wanting to teach but not knowing what my role would be long-term. Each day felt like a moment. Because of this work, I met my husband and best friends. I have seen my former students and even some of their family members become teachers. Over these last 20 years, I have learned more about myself, my privileges and responsibilities, the systems in our society that HAVE to change, and the extraordinary people who are impacting these necessary changes. These moments are what define our roles in this movement!

"There is a certain enthusiasm in liberty that makes human nature rise above itself, in acts of bravery and heroism"- After 20 years, you can imagine the plethora of people whose lives have positively impacted mine. For two decades I have seen people act courageously on behalf of all people and in the name of justice. And, I have seen progress! I write this letter for everyone whose lives I have had the great privilege of working alongside. I am humbled to work with you and grateful for all you do each and every day in pursuit of equity in education.

"There are a million things I haven't done. Just you wait. Just you wait."- I am honored to know that my purpose in life is to be a mom, wife, friend, sister, daughter, community advocate, and teacher coach. I know there is so much to do and be done, and I am elated to continue in this work and hopeful to continue in it alongside many of you!

With Love, Hope, and Liberation,
KP

Lessons and Resources

"If you want to go fast, go alone. If you want to go far, go together" (unknown)
This work gets done not by ourselves but because of the extraordinary people we have alongside us. As I watch the students who served on the school board with me thrive in college, as I watch Dr. Wendy Birhanzel lead a district that

I love so dearly, and even as I write this book and see some of my favorite people in my community running for school board, I am left hopeful for all that is to come because of the people I get to continue working alongside.

Never discount communities at the margins

I am a proud resident of my community. Most of the people who attend school in this district do not look like me nor have backgrounds like mine. Nonetheless, our community, that does happen to be at the "margins" of our city, is making strides. When people really explore our neighborhoods they find people who led the first NAACP in Colorado Springs, entrepreneurs changing the medical career field, a district that is evolving in its understanding of what access and opportunity truly means for students of color and is granting millions of dollars in scholarships and resources to support future students. Our students can graduate from any high school in this area and be guaranteed funds and access to college and opportunities following their K-12 educational careers.

For those who don't live in the community in which you work, I encourage you to at least attend the events. Do your work at the local library. Eat at the local restaurants and relish in the assets of the communities in which your students come from.

Find opportunities to be in positions to invoke change and bring your students along with you

In my role as Deputy Executive Director I, once again,

found myself burned out and walked away from a pretty extraordinary job. I took a step back and realized that just because I was no longer working in the community, did not mean I had to step away from it. After all, I lived there. I realized part of the impetus for my burnout happened to be my relationship with the former superintendent. In this realization, knowing that a change needed to happen for the district, I found my way to the district website where a board vacancy was posted. By finding this vacancy, I had the great opportunity to serve on a board charged with making dramatic change. While my position as a Board Director only lasted approximately one year and five months, I am called back often and continue to serve on one board. Never shy away from those opportunities.

Conclusion

To all the students, friends, family, colleagues, authors, and educators who have taught me,

Thank you for providing me knowledge, love, and growth on this journey. From the students I taught to the teachers I coached, I can arguably say, you all have taught me far more than I likely ever taught you.

In this journey, I have come to realize I don't know everything. In fact, everyone in this world knows so much more than I, especially when it comes to education and justice. In learning this, I am able to grow constantly. In this humility, I have especially learned to look within, confront my biases, and continue to push myself in always being better.

To my students, you were never empty vessels. Yes, I might have known more about fractions, but as a white woman from Colorado, I learned what sweet potato pie was and what it represented in a Southern Black family. What it meant to "stay" somewhere versus "live" somewhere and why that particular distinction meant something to you and your families. I learned what it really meant to potluck in the south on our Thanksgiving with the Pride. I learned what a fade is and the importance of the time spent at the barbershop on a Saturday. I learned to listen and not tokenize and I learned the power of student voice and what it means to truly work toward student liberation in education.

My knowledge, understanding, and humility have grown overtime and especially since becoming a mom. My compassion for students as other people's children has grown immensely as I don't just see students as students but rather someone else's son or daughter. Each human being I have had the great privilege of interacting with is someone else's human, grown from a seed and raised, in most cases, by a family that loves them.

I remember walking into my oldest son Niko's classroom for the first time and worrying who his teacher would be. I have that worry to this day and now wonder, "what did my former students' parents feel when they saw me?" What went through Mark's mom's, Nala's mom's, or Jason's grandma's hearts and minds? Did they worry their child would once again be taught by another white woman who likely had her judgments about Black and Brown kids and would perpetuate thoughts and actions that did not in fact support positive outcomes for their child? Perhaps. I now know in order to end this perpetuation of bias I must surround myself with people who will call me in and confront me if I consciously or unconsciously engage in harmful behavior that does not support our students' liberation. I also know I must continue the inner work to ensure I am cognizant of how I am treating and truly supporting ALL my students toward a life that will guarantee them justice and freedom.

I have learned it is critical to never forget your roots. Three of my toughest years of teaching were my first, third, and seventh. I remember this as I coach teachers, explaining, when they are in funks, it is not just a matter of getting out of it but working *through* it in different ways. I am and always will be a teacher and a teacher who struggled, and while I left the classroom, I have found my way back in sustainable ways. The struggle is real, but it is something we can overcome with support, belief, practice, and healthy habits.

In a poem I wrote as a younger mom I declared: "What my children deserve, all children deserve too." I once thought that having a heart full of love and passion was enough. I eventually learned the "system" is messed up because of people like myself who wanted to change things but weren't looking within to see how they are perpetuating the harmful system. Yes, all children deserve the best and we must continue to do the self-work to ensure we are truly providing equitable opportunities for ALL.

I write this letter in tears knowing this is likely not the last letter I will write but one that concludes these vulnerable and hard to share stories.

As I write this letter, I will leave you with the words and ideals of Richie Reseda, who explains *Abolition Is An Act of Love (2021)*. We cannot actually hold anyone accountable but ourselves. And there are essentially three levels of accountability.

Layer 1: Understanding and acknowledging the harm that I've done.
Layer 2: Committing to never doing it again.
Layer 3: Committing to transforming systems that lead to that kind of behavior in the first place.

In this book, I acknowledge the harm I have done, I commit to never doing these things again, and I am truly committed to transforming systems that led to my harmful behaviors in the first place.

With this, you have my commitment to always be better and continuously being *taught* in support of transformational classrooms and true student liberation.

Thank you for helping me on this journey.

All my love,
Kelley
KP
Ms. Adams
Mrs. Pomis

Acknowledgements

I write this portion with a deep cleansing sigh...

First and foremost, to my beloved students and their families. Thank you for being the source of my inspiration, humility, and on-going development as a white educator in the United States.

To Sia Henry, my editor, who met me with equal parts support and push. You challenged my writing and my thinking. Your passion for equity and editing are invaluable.

To my dearest friends Nikkea Wiler, Anissa Miller, Brandy Nelson, DaKia McCray, Kathy Norwood, Tacha Thebaud, Tasha Brown, Emily White, Ayinde Rudolph, Wendy Birhanzel, Kristi Trangsrud and Velia Rincon. Each of you have had a profound impact on my life, especially as you have lovingly pushed me out of my comfort zone, challenging me to explore my identity as a white woman working in communities of color. You have called me in during my moments of misunderstanding and have created safe spaces for me to be accountable to the privileges I have enjoyed in my life. Without you, there is no way I would have had the words or courage to confront and learn from the harm I have ucaused and ultimately write this book.

To Nicole Amidei and Alison Detviler, you provided me with sacred spaces to disappear for my "writing Me-kends."

To my writing community: Sheela, Shilo, Khristee, Stacy, Lara, Ellen Elizabeth, April, Amanda Louisa, Paola, Crystal, Cathy, Efi and Charity. It has been so fun to be on this journey with you. You have provided me insight, wisdom, and hope. I love and appreciate all of the energy you have gifted me throughout this process.

To Keith Burnam, with all my love to you and all you brought to this world. You saw me through so much of this messiness and my mistakes and yet never gave up on me. I miss you every day!

And to my boys, Aaron, Niko, and Aleko. You are my world. While it might seem that this book has been my world for the last year, you truly are my source of inspiration. Aaron, I have stayed in education because of YOU. As I burned out and contemplated leaving the profession and finding a job I wouldn't have to take home, our conversations and your belief kept me coming back and ultimately staying. Now, twenty years later, here we are... chronicling these stories! And Niko and Aleko, you are my biggest cheerleaders. You are what gets me up in the morning and have fueled my drive for so much in life, especially my fight for educational equity. I love you all so much!

References

Allensworth, E., Ponisciak, S., & Mazzeo, C. (2009). The Schools Teachers Leave: Teacher
    Mobility in Chicago Public Schools. *Consortium on Chicago School Research at the University of Chicago Urban Education Institute.*

Blackwell, F. (1963). [Woolworth's Lunch Counter Sit-In]. *Associated Press.*
    https://www.washingtonpost.com/local/the-lunch-counter-now-has-two-empty-seats-she-is-the-only-one-left-who-can-describe-what-it-felt-like-to-sit-there-that-hateful-day/2019/01/16/f4aecc00-19bd-11e9-9ebf-c5fed1b7a081_story.html.

Choate, J. N. (1885). [Native American Assimilation, Carlisle School]. *Carlisle Indian School*
    Digital Resource Center. https://carlisleindian.dickinson.edu/images/tom-torlino-1882-and-1885.

Commission on Education . (2014). Teacher Turnover: Stayers, Movers, and Leavers . *Digest of*
    Education Statistics.

Condon, F., & Young, V. A. (2017). *Performing Anti-Racist Pedagogy.* Fort Collins: CSU Open
    Press.

Education, U. S. (2011). *Facts about the Teaching Profession* . National Conversation about
    Teaching .

[Elizabeth Eckford's First Day of School: Little Rock Nine]. (1957). *Images, Bettman/ Getty.*
    https://www.history.com/news/the-story-behind-the-famous-little-rock-nine-scream-image.

Freire, P. (2000). *Pedagogy of the Oppressed.* New York: Continuum .

Gershenson, S., Holt, S. B., & Papageorge, N. (2016). Who Believes in Me? The Effect of
    Student-Teacher Demographic Match on Teacher Expectations. *Economics of Education Review.*

Gorski, P. (2019). Avoiding Racial Equity Detours. *Educational Leadership* .

Gray, L., Taie, S., & O'Rear, I. (2015). Public School Teacher Attrition and Mobility in the First
    Five Years: Results from the First Through Fifth Waves of the 2007-2008 Beginning Teacher Longitudinal Study First Look. *US Department of Education.*

Hart, R. (1992). Ladder of Participation .

Hausner, E. (1964). School Boycott. *NY Times.*
    https://www.nytimes.com/2019/03/26/nyregion/school-segregation-new-york.html.

Helms, J. (1990). White Racial Identity Model .

Hudson, R., & Houston, R. (Directors). (2004). *Mighty Times: The Children's March* [Motion
        Picture].

Ingersoll, R. (2018). *The American Teaching Force: Now Covering Three Decades.*

Love, B. L. (2019). Dear White Teachers: You Can't Love Your Black Students if You Don't
        Know Them: Why Loving "All" Students Isn't Good Enough. *Ed Week* .

Meckler, L., & Rabinowitz, K. (2019, December 27). America's schools are more diverse than
        ever. But the teachers are still mostly white. *The Washington Post.*

Miranda, L. M. (2015). *Hamilton.* Rogers Theater, New York , New York .

Moore, C. (1963). [The Children's Crusade]. *The New Yorker.*
        https://www.newyorker.com/news/news-desk/fifty-years-
        after-the-birmingham-childrens-crusade.

Reseda, R. (2021, February 15). Abolition is an Act of Love. *Love Extremist Radio* .

Singh, A. (2019). *The Racial Healing Handbook.* Oakland : New Harbinger Publishing.

Smith, C. (2016). When kids say sorry, are they learning a lesson or just parroting empty words?.
        Greater Good Magazine.

Sutcher, L., Darling-Hammond, L., & Carver-Thomas, D. (2016). A Coming Crisis in Teaching?

Teacher Supply, Demand, and Shortages in the U.S. *Learning Policy Institute*.

[The Day After Brown vs. Board of Education: Nettie Hunt and Daughter]. (1954). *Bettman/ Corbis*. https://pickingatopic.weebly.com/brown-v-board-of-education.html.

[U.S. Army troops escort Little Rock Nine]. (1957). *Everett Collection* . https://upfront.scholastic.com/issues/2017-18/090417/the-little-rock-nine.html#1210L.

[U.S. Marshals escort Ruby Bridges to and from School]. (1960). *Public Domain*. https://www.biography.com/news/african-american-youth-civil-rights-movement.

Wang, K. (2019). Teacher Turnover: Why It's Problematic and How Administrators Can Address It . *The Science of Learning Blog*.

[We Serve White's Only]. (n.d.). *Immigration Impact*. https://immigrationimpact.com/2010/12/14/white-house-to-award-latino-civil-rights-advocate-sylvia-mendez/we-serve-whites-only-no-spanish-or-mexicans/#.YghQ9t_MKM8.

About the Author

Kelley Pomis is wife to Aaron (a fellow educator) and mother to two boys (Niko and Aleko). While she stays busy with her various roles in education, she likes people to know, she is a wife and mom who loves to work.

She is also a veteran educator and host of the Teacher Renewed Podcast. As an expert in teacher development and leadership , she has shared her thinking on the TedX stage as well as having received award recognition in both her community and education .

As a teacher, school administrator, school board member, and teacher coach, Kelley has over two decades of experience helping educators turn classrooms into transformative spaces for both teachers and students. Kelley empowers educators to expand their impact and grow their ability to sustain in this work.

And to everyone who knows Kelley... the mountains are calling and she must go!

Kelley's first day of teaching
August 2002

Kelley's first classroom
The teacher's former smoking lounge